Ningyô: The Art of the Human Figurine

Ningyô

The Art of the Human Figurine

Traditional Japanese Display Dolls
from the Ayervais Collection

With additional pieces from
the Peabody Essex Museum, Salem, Massachusetts,
The Newark Museum and
the Museum of the City of New York

Curated by Gunhild Avitabile

Essay by Shigeki Kawakami
Catalogue entries by Sumie Kobayashi,
Midori Aida and Kohichi Nakamura

Japan Society, Inc., New York, 1995

This catalogue is published in conjunction with the exhibition "Ningyô: The Art of the Human Figurine—Traditional Japanese Display Dolls from the Ayervais Collection, with Additional Pieces from the Peabody Essex Museum, Salem, Massachusetts, The Newark Museum and the Museum of the City of New York," shown at the Japan Society Gallery, New York, from February 17 to April 2, 1995.

The exhibition and catalogue are made possible with funds from the Lila Acheson Wallace/Japan Society Fund, established at Community Funds, Inc. by the co-founder of Reader's Digest; The Japan Foundation; and the Friends of Japan Society Gallery.

Curator: Gunhild Avitabile
Essay: Shigeki Kawakami
Entries: Sumie Kobayashi, Midori Aida, Kohichi Nakamura

Editor: Erica Hamilton Weeder
Translators: Bryce Cunningham for Shigeki Kawakami's essay;
Haruka Hiruta and Morihiro Sato for the entries of S. Kobayashi, M. Aida and K. Nakamura

Designer: Stefanie Krieg-Elliott
Special Consultant: Ayervais
Adviser on traditional Japan: Yasuko Shimizu
Photographs of the Ayervais Collection, unless otherwise indicated, are by Robert Ricke and Ayervais.
Photographs of objects from museums have been supplied by them.

Set in Tiepolo-Book
Text paper: Diadem spezial gestrichen
Offset elementar chlorfrei
Printed and bound in Germany by the Benedict Press, Münsterschwarzach, in an edition of 1,500

Copyright © 1995 Japan Society, Inc.
All rights reserved
Library of Congress Catalogue Card Number: 94-073658
ISBN: 0-913304-41-7

Cover: *Sandai-ningyô* (Court-Visiting *Ningyô*), ca. 1800, no. 41
Frontispiece: *Hina* Stand, 1928, The Newark Museum. Photograph: courtesy of The Newark Museum

Exhibition Design: Gunhild Avitabile, Art Clark
Installation: Jeffrey Nemeth
Brochure: Miwako Nishizawa Glick

Note to the Reader:
Japanese names are printed in the Japanese order, surname first, except in the case of individuals who have chosen to adopt the Western system. In this catalogue, a circumflex is used instead of a macron.

In dimensions listed, height or length precedes width. All measurements are in centimeters.

Contents:

Prefaces: p. 5

Essay: p. 11

Glossary: p. 24

Entries: p. 29

Color section: p. 35

Officers and Directors of the Japan Society, Art Committees and Friends of Japan Society Gallery: p. 95

Gosho-ningyô: Miniature Version with *Eboshi* Hat; ca. 1850, Kyoto

Preface: Deciphering an Unknown World for the West

Ningyô means "human shape or figure." This name seems to be most appropriate to Japan's historical, decorative figurines displayed on various occasions. Best known in the West are figurines called *hina*, "chicks," featured in the *Hina-matsuri*, the Girls' Festival, on March 3. On that occasion, the solemn emperor and empress (usually referred to modestly in Japan as *obina*, "male *hina*," and *mebina*, "female *hina*"), with their elaborate royal household, are arranged on the *hina-dan*, a tiered display stand (nos. 11-27). Also familiar in the West are the warrior figurines for the *Tango-no-sekku*, the Boys' Festival on May 5 (nos. 28-40).

There are many different types of *ningyô* figurines. One type might have been used as auspicious gifts for various occasions; the *gosho-ningyô* (Imperial Palace *ningyô*) of Kyoto, for example, were exchanged as presents by members of the Imperial court and by the court and warrior nobility (*kuge* and *buke*) (nos. 61-81). Another might show customs and beliefs, such as the figurines representing the Ceremony of Attaining Manhood (*gempuku*, no. 43). Others teach us the fashions of their time and are, therefore, important historical documents (nos. 51-53, 55); still others represent roles from famous plays of the Kabuki and Bunraku theater (nos. 44-47). (Puppets of the Bunraku are excluded from this show.) Special types, like Ichimatsu-*ningyô*, were used as dolls for play and strike us today as sensibly executed miniature copies of real children (nos. 82-84). They were often sold naked (*hadaka*) and their young owners were supposed to create clothing for them. *Iki-ningyô* are interesting life-size figurines (no. 85). Beautiful "Friendship Dolls," messengers of peace between children in the United States and Japan in 1927, are another group worthy of our attention (no. 86).

All objects from before the Taishô period (1912-26) in this catalogue and exhibition, with very few exceptions, were created by artistic craftsmen for rich commoners or for members of the nobility living in the great cities, primarily Kyoto and Tokyo. Objects in the exhibition date from the beginning of the 17th century (nos. 1, 2) up to 1993 (no. 86c). A few examples of folk art *ningyô* have been added as reference pieces (Fushimi, Sagara, see pp. 22, 24). Other types, such as the Nara-*ningyô*, kokeshi-*ningyô* or paper dolls (*anesama-ningyô*), were not included.

In the West, the history, development and meaning of these figurines has never before been the subject of extensive studies or of exhibitions based on scholarly research. The few publications in Western languages, written mostly by enthusiastic collectors who very seldom had access to Japanese sources, sometimes present information only about the iconographic meaning of *ningyô*. At times their approach can be counterproductive to the idea of accepting the art of *ningyô* as equal to other artistic craft forms practised in Japan from the Edo period until modern times.

The impact of the West in Japan brought a sharp decline in the art of *ningyô*, but by 1936, it had achieved recognition as an art form. That year, *ningyô* artists participated for the first time in the Nippon Bijutsu Tenrankai, the annual exhibition of the Imperial Art Academy. From the 1930s on, several associations dedicated, and still dedicate, themselves to the study of old and the production of modern *ningyô*. Since 1955, five *ningyô* masters have become designated Intangible Cultural Properties (*mukei bunkazai*), popularly called Living National Treasures: Hirata Gôyô (1903-1981), Hori Ryûjo (1897-1984), Kagoshima Juzô (1898-1982), Noguchi Sonou, born 1907, and Ichihashi Toshiko, born 1907. It is through their work and their recognition that *ningyô* figurines of high quality still preserve their status as artistic display objects.

It seems that our Western society, where easily discarded fantasy turtles or dinosaur figures are complemented primarily by "cute" dolls—all in unbreakable plastic—finds it difficult to cope with the inhabitants of the mysterious, delicate world-in-miniature of Japanese *ningyô*, which are made more for contemplation than for active handling. Unfortunately, it must be admitted that the contemporary toy market is inundated with unbearable kitsch, part of which comes from Japan. Moreover, good toys for children have become luxury objects which can hardly be afforded. Another obstacle to appreciating *ningyô* is related to the fact that "dolls" recently have become, in the eyes of some, symbols of educational conservatism.

It might be true that we find so few collections of Japanese display figurines in the West because they are so delicate. This is also the case for the miniature models of real-world objects that surround them. Materials used to make them are extremely vulnerable when exposed to any uncontrolled environment. Wood, a modeling paste (*tôso*) created by combining sawdust and rice paste (*nerimono*), papier-mâché (*hariko*), silk, cotton, *gofun* (which consists of finely crushed oyster shells mixed with paste, then delicately polished), lacquer, and lacquered-and-gilded paper are just some of the materials used to create these objects (see p. 29). Many figurines may have been destroyed in, or deaccessioned from, Western collections because nobody understood how to conserve or handle them; nor did they appreciate their material value on the art market.

In their home country, *ningyô* have been shown only on special occasions, such as the above-mentioned festivals, or as display objects in a Japanese home—shown for a limited period of time, otherwise wrapped and stored carefully away. *Ningyô* have kept their magical character over the centuries; in fact, when we study these small beings of a magical world, we can understand why many Japanese continue to harbor in their hearts a certain fear of the supernatural power hidden inside of these seemingly realistic human figurines. Nevertheless, as is true in many other countries, the thoughtful admiring and handling of dolls or figurines in human shape, with their

No. 1, Plate I; text, p. 29. Saga-*ningyô*: Young Boy with Little Dog; ca. 1620, Saga

various belongings, have been highly valued for the education of children.

If I would have to compare Japanese display figurines with dignified Western counterparts, I would mention the marvelous crèches of 18th-century Naples, the realistic figurines of Bambino Gesù in South-European churches, or the animated, lifelike saints of the Baroque Hispanic world. Other *ningyô* remind us of fashion figurines of the 18th and 19th centuries, which were highly esteemed miniature messengers from Paris or London to other countries, at a time when communication was less easy than it is today.

Since my first encounter with *ningyô* figurines, I have wished to know more about these strange sculptures which combine a strong decorative element with a hidden magical meaning. Because of the situation described previously, there have been very few occasions to find collections and information. Therefore, I was delighted when the Ayervais Collection, which contains more then a hundred *ningyô* figurines of outstanding quality, was offered for exhibition at Japan Society Gallery.

Collecting Japanese *ningyô* without being a native, traditional Japanese bears some risks. It is always possible to be carried away by a certain Western taste for glittering exoticism. If a collector can get advice from experts, this danger diminishes. Standing on his or her own requires a deep sensitivity for quality and an eye for great art. The owner of this rare collection reveals, in the short preface that follows, the whole complicated and even painful process of "opening one's eyes" to a new world. Nevertheless, to discover something for oneself is a rather common event; to accept the opinion of experts, to go out and share discoveries with others, to help transmit their message—these qualities distinguish the real lover of art. Therefore, my very special and warm thanks go to the owner of the Ayervais Collection, an artist and inventor, who also served as a special consultant for this exhibition.

The preparation turned out to be more difficult than could have been foreseen, especially finding the right experts to transform a private collection into a show which combines aesthetics with educational substance. When I approached Shigeki Kawakami, Curator of the Kyoto National Museum—responsible for textiles and, therefore, also for *ningyô*—at a rather late stage in this project, he agreed with great enthusiasm to write the introductory essay for this catalogue.

I cannot praise enough my three friends from one of the major centers of *ningyô* research in Japan, the Nihon Ningyô Gangu Kai: Sumie Kobayashi, Curator of the Yoshitoku Doll Collection; her sister, Midori Aida; and Kohichi Nakamura, journalist and expert not only of Japanese *ningyô*, but also of European bisque dolls. With great personal sacrifice, they volunteered to come personally to New York City to assist the collector and me by identifying and evaluating the objects in the Ayervais Collection, as well as those from the museums which have lent for this exhibition from their precious holdings.

These two ladies are daughters of one of the most illustrious advocates for a modern appreciation of the old art of *ningyô*: Yamada Tokubei X (1896-1983), the 10th-generation head of the Yoshitoku Ningyô Company, founded in 1711. Together with the poet and painter Takehisa Yumeji (1884-1934) and the painter Nishizawa Tekiho (1889-1965), he promoted the new movement described above. His institute, founded in 1933, gave annual courses for hundreds of professional and amateur *ningyô* makers involving teachers from art academies, painters, scholars of literature and many craftspeople.

I want to warmly thank my colleague Valrae Reynolds, Curator of Asian Art at The Newark Museum and member of the Art Advisory Committee of the Japan Society Gallery, for her support of the project and for her generosity in lending us not only the complete sets of the Girls' and Boys' Festivals (see pp. 2, 28), but also the famous "Miss Osaka," with her siblings and accoutrements (no. 86). This thanks is also extended to Mary Sue Sweeney Price, Director of The Newark Museum. Dan Monroe, Director of the Peabody Essex Museum, Salem, Massachusetts, agreed immediately to send some exquisite *ningyô* from the museum's world-famous collection (nos. 2, 15, 42, 54, 85). Thanks go also to Susan Bean, Curator of Ethnology, and to Christina Behrmann, Assistant Curator of Asian, Oceanic and African Arts and Cultures. With enthusiasm, Ms. Behrmann helped me select pieces from the museum's numerous collections, and arranged, with great care, all necessary steps needed to transfer the treasures to New York. The Museum of the City of New York, generally not involved with Japanese art, lent us the figurine of a courtesan (no. 58), a 1955 gift from the Osaka Steamship Company to the Mayor of New York City in commemoration of the 100th anniversary of Commodore Perry's landing in Japan. We chose this figurine as a contemporary example of the old tradition of giving a *ningyô* as an auspicious gift. I am grateful to Robert R. Macdonald, Director of this museum, and to Sheila Clark, consultant for its toy collection.

Profound thanks go to Mrs. Jirô Murase, whose family has had a long-term relationship with the Japan Society, for her help and advice.

As has been the case in many other exhibitions during these five years that I have been Director of Japan Society Gallery, my special thanks go to my staff and to the staff of the Japan Society, as well as to my freelance collaborators. Yasuko Shimizu, with her broad knowledge of traditional Japan, has helped us in preparing the essay as well as the exhibition. On the Japan Society Gallery staff, I have to mention Elizabeth Rogers, Assistant Director, Miyuki Dellarso, Administrative Assistant, Melissa Rockefeller, part-time collaborator, as well as David Goldenberg and Claudia Bob, student interns. Jeffrey Nemeth installed the exhibition with great care, helped by Ray Tillotsen.

Without my editor and Education Curator, Erica Weeder, it would not have been possible to edit the manuscripts for this catalogue in such a short time. She also helped me plan the educational programs for this show, especially the event at the time of the Girls' Festival, as an effort to bring American and Japanese families closer together.

I am grateful to Bryce Cunningham, who translated Shigeki Kawakami's substantial essay with scrupulous sensitivity. Haruka Hirota and Morihiro Sato receive my thanks for the translation of the catalogue entries provided by Sumie Kobayashi, Midori Aida and Kohichi Nakamura.

My gratitude goes to Robert Ricke and Ayervais, as well as to Roman Szechter, who photographed the objects of the Ayervais Collection. Stefanie Krieg-Elliott designed a splendid catalogue in an extremely short time. Art Clark gave me his valuable support as design consultant for the exhibition. Yuriko Grant helped us to set up the *ningyô* in the proper way.

Last, but not least, Linda Miller, a long-term volunteer at the Japan Society, should be acknowledged for having introduced the marvels of Japanese art to the collector and for having served as his adviser. She deserves our special gratitude because she drew our attention to this marvelous collection.

Gunhild Avitabile
Director, Japan Society Gallery

Hina-matsuri, Gonin-bayashi (Five Musicians), ca. 1840-50, Edo (Tokyo), see no. 21/22, p. 30

The Collector's Preface

Strolling through an antiques show about ten years ago, I found myself drawn to a pair of figurines. They were, the dealer told me, an emperor and empress of the Edo period. Although I had spent innumerable hours in art museums, I had never seen Japanese *ningyô*, and did not know how I (and the museums) could have missed such a brilliant art form. When I left the show, I could not get the emperor and empress out of my mind. Returning to buy them the next day and discovering that someone else now owned them, I felt a great sense of loss and resolved to find another pair.

In fact, I became passionate about *ningyô*. I felt I had discovered an art form unappreciated for its value and importance as great art. To "discover" an art form that has been around for centuries was a humbling experience. I felt like an explorer in a beautiful, superhuman world. It became a challenge to find *ningyô* from Japan's past and to educate myself about them. Since so little has been written about them in English, I had to rely on my eyes and heart as I added piece after piece to my collection.

The *ningyô* for this collection had to have a soul, a certain spirit—the same spirit that exists in any important Western figural study.

I perceive *ningyô* as having the same artistic and historical importance as Western sculpture. Unlike Western sculpture, however, *ningyô* are comprised of many different materials; and I began to study the *gofun*, fabric, carved wood, lacquer—searching for mastery in each medium. The more I examined *ningyô*, the more I needed to learn about them. Who used the wisteria *mon* (family crest)? What did the warrior represent to his country? What sounds did the musicians make? Why are those men in such exaggerated stances? What is the traditional tea ceremony? At what festival or ritual would these dancers have performed? I have been drawn into Japanese history, culture, theater, tea tradition, fashion. There seems no end to the possibilities for research. And yet, each *ningyô* can be appreciated and enjoyed, even if one knows nothing but the joy that beauty can give: *ningyô* as an art form can stand on its own.

It gives me great pleasure to share this collection.

Ayervais

No. 3, Plate II; text, p. 29. *Amagatsu* and *Hôko*; ca. 1780-1800, Kyoto

Ningyô: An Historical Approach

Shigeki Kawakami

The Origin of *Ningyô*

In Japan, artifacts resembling *ningyô* first appeared in the Jômon period, more than 10,000 years ago. At first, stones collected from the banks of rivers were carved to add the impression of hair and breasts, so that they resembled the female form. In time, two-dimensional figurines which displayed shoulders and narrow hips began to be produced, until eventually, over the course of many thousands of years, these figurines became modeled and three-dimensional. It is widely considered that figurines created in the Jômon period were to express magical beliefs.

As we enter the historical periods, the first written records referring to *ningyô* appear in the Heian period (794-1185). In writings of that time, we find mention of the words "*hitogata*," "*amagatsu*" and "*hihina*," respectively—types of figurines which might be viewed as prototypes of those created in later ages. Ancient people read the characters now read as *ningyô*, as *hitogata*—literally, "human form." Originally made of paper and wood and shaped like the human body, *hitogata* served as symbolic substitutes for people, carrying in their stead the burdens of illness and misfortune. These figurines were ritually invested with the pollution which afflicted a person, then set adrift in a river or ocean, to be purified. Even today, the custom of *nagashi-bina* ("wash-away *hina*") is practiced in various locales, preserving this ancient purifying function of *ningyô*.

Amagatsu and *Hôko* (plate II, no. 3)

Amagatsu and *hôko* are types of figurines which express this ancient function of *ningyô*. They were substitutes, placed by the bedsides of infants, to prevent their being afflicted by misfortune.

Amagatsu were already being produced in the Heian period, and are mentioned in both *The Tale of Genji* (*Genji monogatari*; ca. 1000) and *The Tale of Flowering Fortune* (*Eiga monogatari*; 11th century). There are no extant examples of *amagatsu* from before the Middle Ages, but even those made during the Edo period remained faithful to the original designs. *Amagatsu* are made with cylindrical sticks arranged into a T-shape—expressive of a body and arms—onto which a white, silk cloth-covered head is attached.

Hôko are white silk dolls stuffed with cotton. Their production is detailed in a work about childbirth from the Muromachi period entitled, *O-san-no-Kishiki*. The name *hôko* means "crawling baby," and its form represents the crawling posture of an infant. *Hôko* figurines were traditionally made on the same day as the birth of a child, and served as the baby's talismanic substitute.

By the time of the Edo period, these two types of figurines were treated as a pair; *amagatsu* came to represent boys, and *hôko*, girls. They were added to *hina-kazari* (*hina* display), decorative sets of figurines. Since ancient times, these dolls expressed parents' heartfelt prayers for the welfare of their children, a sentiment transcending all divisions of period and class.

Formalization of the Doll Festival (*Hina-matsuri*)

During the Heian period, in addition to *hitogata* and *amagatsu*, there were dolls named *hihina*. *Hihina* is a word which later became associated with the types of dolls used in the Girls' Doll Festival, but it originally denoted a "miniature," or "copy." Thus, what was referred to as *hihina* during this period does not necessarily refer to a *hina* doll, the use of which is now connected to the seasonal festival known as *Hina-matsuri*. This festival evolved from the Chinese practice of cleansing away impurities; it took place early in the third month of the lunar calendar. During the Heian period it was established as a court ritual, which began to be held consistently on March third. However, the practice of enshrining or devoting dolls at these ceremonies was yet to be established. For in *The Tale of Genji*, we find descriptions of young princesses playing with *hihina* dolls, which seems to suggest that dolls were used by children as everyday playthings (see p. 12). Their use was not limited to the *Hina-matsuri*, the "Doll's Festival," as the celebration on March third would come to be known.

Precisely when it became customary to display dolls on March third is uncertain. It seems likely that the use of *hitogata*, tokens for dispelling misfortune, whose use corresponded to the aforementioned seasonal festival of the third month, became identified over time with *hihina*, which were children's playthings. (Eventually, the display of *hina* dolls became part of the ceremony associated with *Hina-matsuri*.) One Muromachi-period diary, the *Oyudono-no-ue-nikki*, kept by the ladies-in-waiting at the Imperial court, contains an entry from March 2, 1530 which details the custom of including *hitogata* along with *hina* dolls, to be sent together as presents. It is likely by then, that the *hina* festival of March third had been established.

After the establishment of the *hina* festival as an official ceremony, dolls underwent a change, becoming increasingly decorative and extravagant. *Hihina*, objects of play, evolved into luxurious and elaborate *hina* dolls. However, during the early part of the Edo period, the practice of displaying such dolls was restricted in large part to the court and to samurai families. Among common families, the display of dolls took place on a considerably smaller scale. During the Genroku era (1688-1704), it was customary among townspeople to display just two or three pairs of dolls on a small stand set in front of miniature folding screens. The appearance of these simple displays

Essay

Tosa Mitsuyoshi (1539-1613): Display of a Doll House; chapter: *Momiji-no-ga, Genji-monogatari kagami*, Izumishi Kubo-so Memorial Museum, Izumi city, Osaka (see p. 30)

can be deduced from two illustrated almanacs published during the Genroku era called *Yamato Kôsaku e-sho* and *Nihon Saijiki* (1688). A reference in *Yamato Kôsaku e-sho* attests to the widespread practice of displaying dolls in Japan: "In this day the display of exact replicas of *dairi-bina* (emperor and empress *hina*), is a practice carried out even in the farthest reaches of Mutsu, the northernmost province of Honshû." During this period, what had originally been an informal practice of displaying dolls became established as a festival, and spread throughout Japan.

By the mid-Edo period, as the practice of *hina-asobi* (playing with dolls) spread to the common classes, its original function of removing pollution was weakened. It became a ceremony in celebration of Girls' Day, at which time parents prayed for the happiness and good health of their daughters. The formalization of the festival is indicated by the fact that it began to be commonly referred to as *Hina-matsuri*, which can be translated as Doll Festival, used interchangeably with Girls' Day Festival, instead of *hina-asobi*, which literally means "playing with dolls."

The Display of Dolls in Edo and the Kyoto-Ôsaka Area (nos. 11-27)

With the establishment of the Dolls' Festival as an official ceremony, the exchange of dolls as presents flourished, as did the production of secondary implements used in doll displays. But as this practice became increasingly ostentatious, the shôgunate responded by intensifying its regulation of such objects. This kind of outward display of wealth by townsmen, particularly by rich merchants, was a cause of great annoyance to the shôgunate; for while merchants were officially regarded as belonging to the lowest social class, their wealth often greatly exceeded the income of samurai. As the Edo period progressed, such material imbalances became an increasingly great source of social tension; thus in the years 1649 and 1658, sumptuary edicts concerning the display of dolls were issued by the shôgunate. In 1721, an order was issued which limited the height of dolls to 24 cm.

Despite the efforts of the shôgunate, the display of figurines became increasingly luxurious. Corresponding to

Small *Dairi-bina*; heads and hands of ivory, 1855, Yoshitoku Collection. Courtesy of Sumie Kobayashi

the increasing number of secondary dolls and implements used in the display of emperor and empress figurines, the number of levels (*dan*) used in the *hina* display stand was also increased. Some *ukiyo-e* prints of the period contain scenes of commoners, who lived in crowded row-houses, using overturned *tansu* chest drawers as makeshift platforms for such displays. During the middle of the 18th century, displays were commonly made up of two or three tiers, but during the latter part of the century, constructions of four, even five, tiers appeared. By the time of the Tempô era (1830-44), magnificent displays reaching seven and eight levels were not unusual. The arrangement of such displays also became formalized; on the top level were placed the *dairi-bina* (nos. 11-13, 16) emperor and empress figurines, while on the lower levels were ladies-in-waiting (no. 20), groups of musicians (nos. 21, 22) and attendants (no. 23). On the right side of the display, stood a miniature cherry tree; on the left, an orange tree. Implements in gold and silver *makie* technique (sprinkled gold and silver lacquer), imitating those used by *daimyô* (feudal lords), were also included.

This trend towards increasing extravagance, conspicuous in cosmopolitan Edo, was not paralleled in the ancient capital of Kyoto. According to the 19th-century *Morisada mankô* (Aimless Drafts of Morisada), a book about Edo-period fashions, the number of levels used in Kyoto and Ôsaka doll displays, in contrast to those of Edo, did not increase but remained limited to two. On the top level, inside a miniature palace, were installed a pair of emperor and empress figurines (no. 15). Unlike the extravagances of Edo, the implements used in Kyoto displays were considerably more modest. The inclusion of everyday kitchen utensils was also in marked contrast to Edo. It is said that this practice stemmed from the characteristic values of Kyoto-area culture, which sought to teach children frugality and to accustom them to tools used for household chores; in the early Shôwa era (around 1930), doll displays were even equipped with kitchens.

However, in recent times, the form of doll displays has become standardized, to the extent that the differences between Edo and Kyoto styles can no longer be distinguished (see frontispiece, p. 2). The standard display at present is as follows: the Imperial figurines are placed on the top level, flanked on both sides by two paper lanterns and a pair of papier-mâché dogs (*inu-hariko* or *inu-bako* [no. 4, plate VI]); between the two Imperial figurines, a stand with bottles of ceremonial sake is placed; behind the Imperial figurines are two small *byôbu*, or folding screens. On the first level beneath, are three ladies-in-waiting (no. 20); and on the next lower level, a group of five musicians (nos. 21, 22, p. 8). In the middle of the fourth level is a ceremonial stand for meals, flanked by two attendants. Various implements are placed on the fifth level. On the right side of the sixth level is a toy cherry tree, and on the left, an orange tree; between these trees are three retainers. Arranged on the bottom level are palanquins and other vehicles (no. 26). After the great Tokyo earthquake of 1923, this standardized type of display began to be sold in department stores.

Arrangement of Male and Female Dolls (nos. 11-16)

Although the arrangement of doll displays became standardized in the Shôwa era, the placement of the emperor and empress figurines took opposite forms in Tokyo and Kyoto. While in the Tokyo style, the emperor figurine was placed on the left (viewing the display from the front), in the Kyoto style, this figurine was located to the right of the empress.

The Kyoto style followed the spatial orientation of the Imperial Palace, in which the highest seat of honor was located to the east (and therefore to the right). In Tokyo, however, after the Meiji Restoration of 1868, court customs and the style of palace architecture became increasingly Westernized: the position of the emperor's throne in the Tokyo palace was reversed. The positioning of the Imperial figurines was changed correspondingly. It appears that this practice became widespread after Emperor Shôwa's ceremonial accession to the throne in 1928, and has continued to the present.

Any attempt to discern the style of arrangement during the Edo period leads us to again consult the two Genroku-period works: the *Nihon Saijiki* (1688) and the *Yamato Kôsaku e-shô*. From pictures contained therein, pairs of standing (*tachibina*) or sitting figurines (*suwari-bina*) can be seen on low stands in front of folding screens. The male figurine was placed on the right. Viewing illustrations in two books published shortly thereafter, the *Ehon Yamato Warabe* (1716-1735) and *Hina-asobi kaiawase-no-ki* (1749), seated figurines are shown with the male placed on the left; while in arrangements of standing figurines, the male is alternately on either side. The illustrations from these books were executed by Nishikawa Sukenobu (1671-1750), a famous master of *ukiyo-e* prints who was active in Kyoto. He was the premier illustrator of books depicting the manners and customs of the day; yet figurines in Sukenobu's drawings are placed in the Tokyo style. Because of such variation, it seems that there was no established form for the presentation of figurines during the mid-Edo period.

Utagawa Kunisada. Young Woman with Emperor and Empress; woodblock print, 1858. Courtesy of Sumie Kobayashi.

However, as doll displays of the late Edo period grew more and more extravagant, in Kyoto the custom of installing the Imperial figurines in a miniature palace seems to have begun (no. 15). These palaces were modeled upon the Shishinden Palace (Hall for State Ceremonies) and were flanked by a cherry tree to the left and an orange tree to the right. As would befit his placement in the Palace, the emperor figurine took his place to the right. In Kyoto, this traditional arrangement is preserved to the present day.

Evolution of *Hina* Figurines (nos. 11-16)

Let us return to our discussion of *hina* figurines of the Edo period. As the Doll's Festival grew more magnificent, the commercialization of *hina* figurines accelerated, and many types began to be manufactured.

Two major classifications of *hina* figurines exist: *tachibina* and *suwari-bina*. *Tachibina* ("standing doll") are modeled after an erect human figure. Male figurines generally have arms extended at their sides and are dressed in short-sleeved kimono called *kosode*, over which are pleated trousers known as *hakama* (Plate III, nos. 9, 10). Female figurines are constructed in a simple cylindrical form, and their *kosode* are tied with a narrow sash like an obi. Made of paper, *tachibina* are also referred to as *kamibina* ("paper doll"). These largely two-dimensional standing figures seem to have conserved many characteristics of ancient forms, in evidence since the Heian period. Needless to say, the Heian form has not been completely preserved; rather, figurines garbed in *kosode* reflect styles current during the Muromachi period. Whatever the case may be, these figurines retain many characteristics of the ages which preceded the Edo period.

It is impossible to confirm with any exactitude the nature of figurines predating the Edo period, but a portrait of Maeda Kikuhime, preserved at Saikyoji temple in Shiga prefecture, contains illustrations of such pre-Edo dolls. Kikuhime was the sixth daughter of Maeda Toshiie (1538?-1599), and she was later adopted by Toyotomi Hideyoshi (see no. 34). She died at the age of seven in 1584, the same year this painting was executed as a memorial. Viewing this image, we see arranged in front of her a papier-mâché dog, toy top and three dolls. Because the form of these dolls is similar to the later *tachibina* style, it is possible that Edo-period *tachibina* dolls represented a development in this trend. From this portrait we may also infer that this type of doll served as a toy for children, rather than as a standing, decorative figurine. As *hina* figurines came to be appreciated for their aesthetic qualities, *suwari-bina* ("sitting doll") which were more stable and therefore easier to display, gained the greatest popularity.

Jirôzaemon-bina; ca. 1751; owned by Zaidan Hojin, Honma Museum, Sakata city Yamagata prefecture

The first type of *suwari-bina* was referred to as *Muromachi-bina*. Miyagawa Nagaharu (1681-1752), the Edo-period *ukiyo-e* master, painted a series entitled "*Hina* Dolls of the Muromachi Period," (*Muromachi-ke-no-Koro-no-Hina-zu*), in which such dolls are featured. Later, the artist Santô Kyôden (1761-1816) took up the same subject in an illustrated work on the manners and customs of the early Edo period, *Kottoshû* (1814-15). These dolls are characterized by their round heads and simple features. Male dolls are clothed in ancient court robes (*sokutai*), while female dolls have *kosode* over *hakama* trousers. Their posture of outstretched arms, with *kosode* sleeves covering their hands, leads us to believe that they were developed from *tachibina* dolls. Among the various types of *suwari-bina*, *Muromachi-bina* displayed a traditional style, but it cannot be confirmed whether or not they were actually manufactured in the Muromachi period. Among the few existing examples of *Muromachi-bina*, all were produced during the Edo period. In any event, it is helpful to consider the title "Muromachi" as expressive of a traditional form and mode of dress.

It is most probable that the style of *suwari-bina* was formalized after the beginning of the Edo period. As several figurine types appeared, from *Kanei-bina*, to *Genroku-bina*, and finally to *Kyôho-bina* (no. 11), *suwari-bina* gradually took their final form. The names of these figurines do not correspond exactly to the reign periods from which they take their names, but it may be considered that their development roughly followed this progression.

Among extant Edo-period *suwari-bina*, those expressive of the most ancient style are *Kanei-bina*, figurines which take their name from the Kanei era (1624-44). Male figurines stand just under 12 cm in height, and wear court robes and lacquered court caps. The heads of these dolls were constructed together with the extending cap, and later painted in black. Females were a size smaller and lacked hands. Both in their posture of out-stretched arms and in their facial expressions, these figurines resemble *tachibina*. However, they are more three-dimensional and naturalistic. As the name *Kanei-bina* suggests, this type of figurine appeared relatively early in the Edo period. Yet even in a

Hina-matsuri/Girls' Festival

No. 9, Plate IIIa, text, p. 29. *Hina-matsuri*: *Tachibina*; ca. 1800, Western Japan

No. 10, Plate IIIb, text, p. 29. *Hina-matsuri*: *Tachibina*; ca. 1880, Kyoto

1732 book on the subject of women's styles, *Onna fûzoku tama-kagami*, illustrated by Nishikawa Sukenobu, we find pictures of displays of *Kanei-bina*. It may be deduced that this type of figurine was very popular, and was displayed continuously over a long period of time.

Genroku-bina (era: 1688-1704) display a form which seems transitional between *Kanei-bina* and *Kyôho-bina* (era: 1716-36). The one-piece construction of the head and court cap, characteristic of *Kanei-bina*, continues, but *Genroku-bina* are one size larger. In addition, female dolls are constructed with hands, and rather than wearing *kosode*, they are dressed in the twelve-layer kimono style (*jûni hitoe-fû*). Both of these factors characterize the later *Kyôho-bina* type of figurine.

By the mid-Edo period, the Doll's Festival began to flourish, and *hina* figurines became larger and more luxurious. The handsome *Kyôho-bina* which appeared during this time had oval faces with long, narrow eyes. Both male and female figurines had naturalistic hair made of silk strands, and were adorned in gorgeous clothes of richly colored, embroidered brocade. Male figurines were dressed in garments which recalled ancient court dress, while female figurines had the twelve-layer-style of kimono, with highly ornate crowns of metal, far from imitating actual Imperial apparel.

After a time, figurines called *Jirôzaemon-bina* (see p. 14) came into fashion. These took their name from Hinaya Jirôzaemon of Kyoto, a famous dollmaker who enjoyed the patronage of the shôgunate. The elegant expression of these round-headed figurines, characterized by long, almond-shaped eyes, small noses and tiny pursed mouths, evokes the Heian-period figure painting style of *hikime kagihana*—literally, "dash-eyes, hook-nose." At first, this type of figurine was used by members of the Kyoto elite, but after 1761 (Hôreki 11), they began to be sold in Edo and soon gained tremendous popularity among all classes.

Not long after the introduction of *Jirôzaemon-bina* into Edo, came the appearance of a new type of doll called *Kokin-bina* (no. 16). It is said that they were first manufactured during the Meiwa era (1764-72) by the Edo dollmaker, Hara Shûgetsu. These dolls supposedly were given the title "Kokin," a name taken from the Heian-period anthology of poems, *Kokinshû*, to designate their appropriate use for girls. According to financial records of a dollmaker's association called Hina Nakama Kôyo-chô, from March 1790 (Kansei 2), *Kokin-bina* had appeared on the market about twenty years previously. It also becomes clear that during the Kansei era (1789-1800), the heads of these dolls were carved in Edo and then shipped to Kyoto to be painted. Male dolls wear court robes, while females wear twelve-layer kimono. In contrast to *Jirôzaemon-bina*, *Kokin-bina* have more naturalistic features, a fact which seemed to match the tendency of late-Edo-period fashion. These figurines were enthusiastically received in Edo and became more fashionable than *Jirôzaemon-bina*. In a comical poem in *haiku* form (*senryû*) from the Bunka era (1804-18), we find the phrase, "Grandma's *Jirôzaemon*, mother's *Kyôho-bina*, the bride's *Kokin-bina*." From this, it is possible to deduce that while *Jirôzaemon-* and *Kyôho-bina* had been popular in previous generations, the *Kokin-bina* had become the new, most fashionable doll. Because of its popularity, many similar figurines came to be produced in Edo—all of which have come to be referred to as *Kokin-bina*. Most figurines produced since the Meiji period seem to have followed the trend of *Kokin-bina*.

Among court nobles, a type of figurine called *yûsoku-bina* was popular; it faithfully reproduced the aristocratic style of dress. Depending on the type of dress, these figurines were named *sokutai-bina*, *nôshi-bina*, *konôshi-bina* or *kariginu-bina*. In the diary of the noble Nonomiya Sadaharu (*Nonomiya Sadaharu Kyôki*), there is an entry of February 10, 1758 (Hôreki 8) which mentions this type of figurine. It seems that families who produced and supplied garments to the court and aristocracy began to manufacture these types of figurines. Not only were they familiar with the designs of the dress, but they used pieces of cloth, leftover from the manufacture of garments, to make outfits.

Sokutai-bina were figurines which accurately represented the formal dress of the nobility. Depending upon its rank, a male figurine is dressed in either a red or black robe closed with a *sekitai* obi; on its head is placed a lacquered cap. In the right hand it holds a scepter, and a sword (*tachi*) is worn at its side. The female equivalent wears what is known as a twelve-layer kimono, or *jûni hito-e*. This style of dress consists of layer after layer of different colored silks, producing a beautiful harmony of colors. The outermost layer, a short colorful silk jacket, is called a *karaginu* ("Chinese" jacket). At the waist is tied a long train, that flows out behind the figure. In the hand is a painted fan of cypress wood. This type of figurine does not have a crown in the style of *kokin-bina*; instead, the hair is pleated from the center of the forehead and bound at the nape of the neck into a long, flowing ponytail style called *osuberakashi*—which is affixed with an ornamental hairpin (*saishi*) and comb.

Nôshi figurines are faithfully represented in the everyday attire of court nobles. Although a less formal everyday style, it was like that worn by the emperor. Therefore, it was still considerably formal and ostentatious. In addition, it was a style worn by Imperial princes and nobles of the upper three ranks who had received the emperor's permission to enter the Palace wearing this apparel, without having to change into a more formal costume. Male figurines wear, for example, white robes and black lacquered caps (*eboshi*) as a winter outfit. Female dolls also wear lighter clothing called *uchigi-hakama* instead of the twelve-layer kimono. *Konôshi* dolls, less formal in their mode of dress than *nôshi*, wear the style of apparel used for outings by high-ranking ministers and generals during the Heian period. This consists basically of a hunting outfit, onto which is stitched a decorative hem, or *ran*, which gives a more formal appearance. Women wear *uchigi-hakama*, sometimes in a style called *kaidori*, for variation. These types of *hina* are not represented in this show and are extremely rare.

Boys' Day Dolls (nos. 28-40)

While the celebration of the Dolls' Festival for girls falls on March third, Boys' Day (*Tango-no-sekku*) is held on May fifth. From ancient times, irises were dedicated to dispel malice and pray for sound health. It was not until the Edo period that dolls began to be displayed as a part of this festival. In an illustrated almanac from the Genroku era (*Yamato kosaku e-shô*), it is detailed how fences in front of houses were constructed, outside of which *ningyô*, armor (*kabuto*), and colorful banners (*nobori*) were displayed. The *Teitoku Kyôka-shû*, a book of *kyôka* (comic *tanka* poems) published in 1682 and illustrated by Hishikawa Moronobu (?-1694), reveals scenes of the dollmaker's section of Edo, which is having a big sale for this festival. It is also evident that by this time warrior dolls were already popular for this occasion. During this period, dolls were displayed on the porch or veranda of houses so that pedestrians could also see them.

By the late Edo period, this display of dolls on verandas seems to have gone out of fashion; instead, it became fashionable to display such dolls in the *zashiki*, or drawing room of a house. In these *zashiki* displays, small decorative banners and two types of spears—one wrapped in a cloth sack, the other topped with feathers—were arranged on a small platform (no. 29). Figurines as well as a set of armor were placed in front of this arrangement (see p. 28). The display of warrior-type dolls was especially popular in Edo with its large population of samurai families. By the end of the Edo period, however, this practice was popular in Ôsaka as well. There, warrior dolls, as well as dolls which represented heroes from Chinese and Japanese history and myth (similar to those in this exhibition), were sold (nos. 28-40). This trend is recorded in a glossary of famous places in Ôsaka, *Settsu meisho zu-e taisei*. These various types of dolls were used until the Meiji and Taishô periods, but following the changes of the times, dolls fashioned in the image of the child-hero Kintarô (no. 39) became the most popular.

The Emergence of Dollmakers

In addition to *hina* and Boys' Day figurines, production of those having no connection to such festivals, but which were suited instead to play, expanded after the beginning of the Edo period.

Of course such dolls were produced prior to the Edo period. In a copy of a screen known as the Machida-family version, which is believed to represent the oldest example of a *rakuchû-rakugai byôbu* (a pair of screens with scenes of Kyoto and its environs) from the period of 1525-36, we can see shops where dolls are being sold. In another version, the so-called Uesugi-family version of the Tembun era

Ningyô Display for the Vienna World Exhibition; 1873. The exhibition started in May; therefore, these display objects are primarily for the Boys' Festival

Photograph: courtesy of Tokyo National Museum

No. 2, Plate IV; text, p. 29. Saga-*ningyô*: Young Boy with Bird; ca. 1620, Saga, Peabody Essex Museum

(1532-55), there appears to be a store selling a simple type of doll which look like *hôko*. Furthermore, in the diary (*Tokitsune kyôki*) of Yamashina Tokitsune (1507-79), it is recorded that on September 15, 1595, Tokugawa Ieyasu (1543-1616) commissioned a doll. Then in the later entry of September 24, it is written that two dolls, manufactured by Eya Utanosuke, were delivered. One of these is a boy doll pulling a dog on a leash, the other is a mechanical-doll drummer. The maker of these dolls, Eya Utanosuke, was originally a painter of the Tosa school, famous for the *Yamato-e* style of painting. This is why he is referred to in his title as a painter (*eya*) instead of dollmaker. Besides making dolls, he was involved in painting fans, and producing decorative paper for poems. Because of his mastery of different decorative crafts, his dolls were beautifully colored.

It is not clear whether or not professional dollmakers existed during the Momoyama period (1573-1614), but in 1690, the third year of the Genroku era, a book *Jinrin-kimmô-zui* (Illustrated Book on Morals and Lifestyles) was published, which lists two categories of dollmakers: *ningyô-shi* and *hina-shi*. *Ningyô-shi* made various kinds of dolls which included *ayatsuri-ningyô* (hand-manipulated puppets), *yubi-ningyô* (finger dolls), *harinuki-ningyô* (hollow papier-mâché dolls), *ishô-ningyô* (costume dolls), *keshi-ningyô* (miniature dolls). On the other hand, the makers of *hina* dolls also made heads for *hôko* dolls which were sold to doll stores.

It seems that within a century after the close of the Muromachi period, there appeared those who earned their livelihood either by making, or dealing in, dolls. It is possible to deduce that the dollmaking process had become more specialized, with various doll parts being produced by specific artisans, and also that the production of dolls had become more commercialized. From the Momoyama to early Edo period, dolls had been manufactured by craftsmen like Eya, who produced dolls as a side job; eventually some of these artisans solely made dolls. This specialization was possible because the demand for dolls during the Edo period greatly expanded.

Saga-*ningyô* (p. 6, no. 1; p. 18, no. 2)

Saga dolls appeared during the early Edo period. These were carved of wood, on top of which layers of *gofun* were applied. After this, they were richly decorated with gold leaf, gold painting and mineral pigments. Because of this complex technique of layering *gofun* (see p. 29) and the rich, detailed coloring, it has been suggested that Saga dolls were created by professional carvers of Buddhist images (*busshi*) during their spare time. There is no evidence which directly supports this theory, but Saga dolls have an unusually sophisticated decorative style and have been greatly appreciated for their beauty. It is possible that makers of Buddhist images made dolls as a sideline, just as the painter Eya did.

Among early dolls, those commonly produced included images of Hotei, so-called *karako* ("Chinese child"), and

Hotei with Children; Saga-*ningyô*, 18th c., private collection

children holding a dog or bird. The smiling faces of these dolls have a unique expression and possess a mysterious charm. Looking at the child dolls, one can see that the collars of their undergarments are tightly closed around the neck, and that a wave-crest motif is frequently used on their clothing. Within the space of the primary figurative pattern of waves or ginko leaves, there is also more superficial decorative patterning, such as a tiny turtle-shell design, called *Bishamon-kikko*, as well as an undulating, vertical serpentine band called *tachiwaki* design. A type of *kosode* dress utilizing this pattern was very popular in the early Edo period, and it is probable that these dolls were made during the same general time (Kanei-Kambun eras, 1625-62).

Eventually, Saga dolls evolved from the specific themes discussed above and began to adopt those related to popular figures of street performance such as monkey trainers, puppeteers and puppets. Manufacture of these dolls also began to be carried out in Edo as well as Kyoto. Saga dolls, which had originally been short and stocky became slender and tall, but the sophisticated technique used to construct and color these dolls was continued, enabling them to retain their elegant appearance.

Saga dolls also include *hadaka* Saga or "naked Saga," representing the unclothed forms of children. The proportions of tiny, young bodies were reproduced realistically, in appreciation of their loveliness. These dolls were already being made in the early part of the Edo period, and it is said that they influenced the development of *gosho-ningyô*.

Gosho-*ningyô* (nos. 61-81)

Created in the image of cherubic children, these dolls are characterized by their large heads, round bodies and brilliant white skin—created by the application of many layers of polished *gofun*. After the Meiji period, this type of doll was called *gosho*. Before then, they were referred to variously as "white chrysanthemum" (*shira-kiku*) or "white

Children Playing; fan-shaped sutra (*Hokke-kyo*); scroll no. 7, eighth fan, bottom illustration; copied after the Heian-period original by Kobori Tomoto (1864-1931), Meiji period, Tokyo National Museum

flesh" (*shirajishi-ningyô*) because of their pure white skin tone, or simply as "large head" (*zudai*). Assuming the name of an Ôsaka doll wholesaler, Izukuraya Kihei, they were also called Izukura dolls.

The childlike proportions of these dolls were formalized between the mid- and late-Edo period. Influencing this formalization were dolls called *hadaka* Saga, or "naked Saga" dolls, which portrayed children's naked forms. *Hadaka* Saga were preserved in Kyoto and Nara in temples headed by a priest-prince. From the early Edo period on, these dolls were loved by aristocratic nuns, who were relatives of the emperor and empress. After a time, this doll was simplified into its characteristic infantlike proportions (three times the head length), becoming more and more charming. It is believed that *gosho-ningyô* evolved in this way. Also, if we observe their eyes, we find that those of early *gosho-ningyô* were long and narrow, resembling those of *hadaka* Saga, but that they gradually became larger and the upper eyelid rounder, giving them an open-eyed expression.

Once the form of *gosho-ningyô* was established, they expressed different themes. Among the varieties of *gosho* were the *haihai*, or "crawling" form (nos. 70, 73), or those who innocently stretched out their limbs. There also were dolls which rode on the backs of turtles, as well as those which beat drums (nos. 67, 69), carried a hobby horse (nos. 63, 65), or held cranes or red snappers in celebration of good fortune. Some *gosho* dolls are dressed. All types expressed the pure, innocent loveliness of children.

Among *gosho-ningyô* are those which have patterns on their foreheads called *mizu-hiki-de* ("red-ribbon style," no. 75). It is said that this patterning originated after *gosho-ningyô* were sent by *daimyô* (feudal lords) as presents to the court. *Mizu-hiki* are decorations of red and white silk cord attached like ribbons to presents; a painted image of *mizu-hiki* was applied as the symbol of its being a gift. The origin of this *mizu-hiki* pattern has also been linked to the decorative silk cords which were used to tie back the hair of the forehead. In any event, the glow of this slender red *mizu-hiki* against the doll's white skin produces a beautiful, contrasting effect.

Some dolls, although they displayed a childlike form, referred to historical or mythical figures, and to characters from Nô plays (*mitate*; parody, no. 74). For example, a figurine wearing a Chinese crown and offering shoes in his left hand would be symbolic of the Chinese hero Chôryô. If a figurine was wearing a lion-head mask and holding in both hands a peony, it would be representing an actor in the Nô play, *Shakkyô* (Stone Bridge). Through this practice of displaying figures of heroes and sages, it was hoped that children would grow up to become outstanding individuals.

In addition to dolls representing Nô characters, there were those dressed in *kosode* and *hakama*, which were intended to look like the children of either samurai (nos. 76, 77) or townspeople (nos. 80, 81); those dressed in *kosode* were meant to resemble young girls. Dolls depicting older children also appeared. Hairstyles of standing figurines faithfully represented those worn by youths of noble families (no. 79) prior to their coming-of-age ceremonies when they reached fifteen (see no. 43).

It is said that *gosho-ningyô* originated in Kyoto because Court nobles who wished for the birth of an heir would donate them as presents to the emperor. It is believed that this is why most *gosho-ningyô* are boys. *Gosho* dolls were invested with the dreams and expectations that noblemen wanted to pass on to their sons, who would carry on the family line. In these plump forms, overflowing with vitality and health, was the hope that children would grow up to become healthy, splendid individuals. Perhaps, more basically, *gosho-ningyô* reflect an essential aspect of the Japanese sense of beauty, which is an appreciation of young children (see ill. above). This sentiment is expressed in *The Pillow Book* (*Makura-no-Soshi*; ca. 1000) of Sei Shônagon: "A very plump baby around two years old or so with fair skin, in indigo blue transparent clothes, too large, tied up with a string so he won't trip, just about crawling out of his room, is cute."

Ishô-ningyô of the "Floating World" (nos. 49-55)

The Genroku era (1688-1703) in which Ihara Saikaku (1642-1693) of Osaka, who chronicled the Floating World, began to gain acclaim, and in which the *ukiyo-e* artist Hishikawa Moronobu was active, was a period which saw the rise of secular activities. It was a time of worldliness and absorption in the swirling, transient world of pleasures. Saikaku's *Tales of an Amorous Man* (*Kôshoku ichi-dai otoko*) describes *ishô* dolls created to resemble high-class courtesans: "He brought twelve long trunks (*nakabitsu*) and took the *ishô-ningyô* out. These dolls represent famous courtesans—seventeen from Kyoto, eight from Edo, and nineteen from Ôsaka—lined up as though they were on stage, each with a name tag." *Ishô-ningyô*, as the name implies, are costumed dolls, but most of the time they represent famous courtesans, beauties, or the female

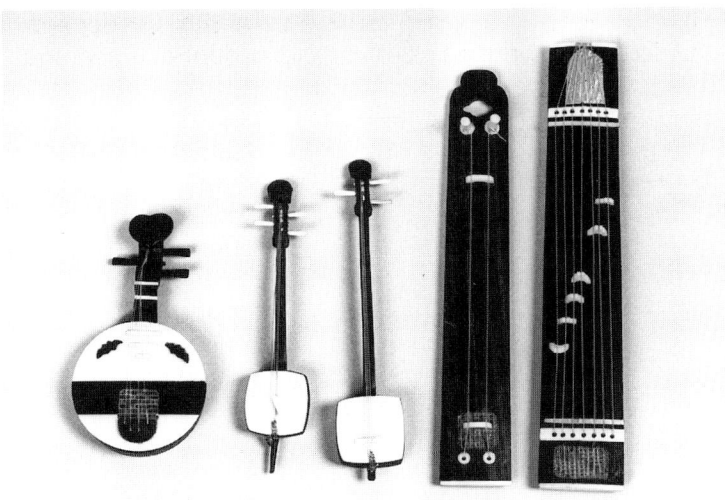

Musical Instruments for the *Hina* Stand

impersonators of Kabuki theater. Because these were all fashionable figures of the entertainment districts, these dolls were sometimes called *ukiyo-ningyô* dolls. It should also be noted that these figurines are important as documents of the fashions of their time because they faithfully reproduced the quickly changing styles of hair and garments.

Ishô-ningyô which represented beauties (*bijin*) of the mid-Edo period, had heads constructed together with hair, then painted. Hairstyles popular at the time can be determined; especially desirable was a hairstyle called Shimada-*mage*. It was first worn by courtesans at a place called Shimada on the Tôkaidô; afterwards, it became popular among young women in the cities. The early Shimada style is fairly simple in comparison to later versions. According to an illustrated book of women's fashion, *Onna-yô kummô-zui* (Women's Illustrated Educational Handbook on Lifestyle), published in 1687, the hair should not be high in front, nor too full on the sides. Women's eyebrows, according to a 1692 edition of a handbook for women's dress and grooming (*Onna chôhôki*), were centered; around them was painted the shape of a crescent moon, which grew lighter at the sides. This ideal of fashion was also reflected in *ishô-ningyô*. If we are to turn our attention to the dress of these dolls, we find that they wear coatlike kimono (*uchikake*) tied with narrow obi, a mode of dress popular during this time.

During this time, when homosexuality was popular, there were also *ishô-ningyô* dolls which represented *wakashû* (female impersonators of early Kabuki theater, who were also male prostitutes). It is apparent from both Saikaku's sequel to the novel, *Tales of an Amorous Man, II* (*Kôshoku nidai Otoko*), as well as Yûkiya Raiji's popular journal of Edo's red-light district, *Shin Yoshiwara tsunezune gusa* (Everyday in the New Yoshiwara), both published 1684 (Teikyo 1). We find mention of a Kyoto dollmaker named Yamada Geki, who gained acclaim by fashioning these *ningyô* of *wakashu*. These dolls, with their oval faces, seem to reflect the taste of the mid-Edo period.

Variations of *Ishô-ningyô*

Ukiyo dolls were not the only type of *ishô-ningyô*, other dolls which emphasized attractive physical appearance were also produced. These included charming types such as children playing with balls, or the Seven Gods of Good Fortune, depicted sitting and stretching out their legs.

Particularly small, even among *ishô-ningyô*, were *keshi-ningyô*. The name *keshi* comes from "poppy seed," and came to refer not only to *ishô* dolls, but to miniature dolls of other sorts as well. There are many examples of dolls between 5 and 10 cm in size; but in the late Edo period the techniques employed by artisans became more refined, and even smaller dolls appeared. Although tiny, they are full of expressiveness.

Another type is *kezukuri-ningyô*, which usually depicted small animals such as dogs and rabbits. *Kezukuri* means "made with hair," and the fur of these dolls is created by attaching hundreds of tiny silk strands. Just like *keshi* dolls, these small figures seem expressive of the Japanese adoration of small, attractive objects.

A type of doll which resembles the *keshi* doll is the variety known as *saiku-ningyô*. These *ningyô* were made as a hobby by amateurs. Lead was affixed to the soles of their feet for weight, and they were clothed. Although not objects of technical virtuosity, they possess a certain warmth and charm. The above-mentioned *ningyô* are not represented in this catalogue.

One type is referred to as Takeda-*ningyô* (nos. 44-47). These were copied after the famous puppet theater of Takeda Izumo at Dotonburi, Ôsaka, popular around the year of 1662. The exaggerated expressions of these dolls evoke the atmosphere of an original theatrical experience.

Mitsu-ore; Three-Fold Dolls (nos. 77, 78, 82-84)

The enjoyment to be had from dolls lies not just in viewing them, but also in holding and fondling them, and changing their clothes. Representative of a type where this is possible are *mitsu-ore-ningyô*. *Mitsu-ore*, meaning "three-way fold," can be bent at the hip, knee and ankle, allowing them to sit. According to a book on fashion and customs called *Morisada mankô* (see p. 13), naked dolls with bending hips appeared in the Anei era (1772-81). Before that, around the Kampô era (1741-44), dolls modeled on the image of the Kabuki actor, Sanogawa Ichimatsu (1722-1763), were fashionable and were referred to as Ichimatsu dolls. It is not known for certain whether Ichimatsu dolls of this period had three joints. Later, however, three-fold dolls which did not resemble the actor Ichimatsu also began to be called Ichimatsu dolls. These dolls have many outfits, which can be changed according to the season, and they are equipped with eating utensils. They are treated lovingly by their owners, who care for them as if they were real children. Later, a male-and-female pair of these dolls was included in the *Hina-matsuri* display.

Toyohara Kunichika. Woman Dressing an Ichimatsu-*ningyô* (*Mitsu-ore*); woodblock print, 1878. Courtesy of Sumie Kobayashi

No. 82: *Mitsu-ore* Construction

Karakuri Dolls (nos. 65-67)

Karakuri-ningyô are mechanical figurines which move by means of springs, sand, mercury, and other devices. At first these dolls were simple objects, capable of moving only their hands and feet. As time went on, interest in such dolls rose. From two illustrated books titled the *Karakuri Kimmô Kagami-gusa* (1730) and *Karakuri-zui* (1796), it can be seen that elaborate *karakuri-ningyô* were produced.

Karakuri were of two varieties: those affixed to stands in which the mechanism for moving the doll was installed, and those which contained a mechanism within the doll itself, allowing it to move independently. In the case of the former, by rotating a handle on the side of the stand it was possible to make the doll play the *shamisen* or to turn around in circles. Others of this type had a black box filled with sand attached to the back of the doll's stand; by turning the box up or down, the sand would fall in the manner of an hourglass. This force would then animate the doll to perform its antics.

Representative of dolls that can move independently are somersaulting dolls, or those which carry and serve wine or tea. In the case of somersaulting dolls, mercury is contained within the body. Because of the movement of this substance, the figurine's center-of-gravity changes and it somersaults, tumbling down stairs. For wine-carrying *ningyô*, the weight of a cup set into the *ningyô*'s hands triggers a wire in the figurine, which sends it forward on a tiny wheel mechanism, making it look as if the doll were walking forward to serve the wine.

Kamo-*ningyô* (nos. 5-8)

The body of a Kamo-*ningyô* was carved in one piece out of willow wood. Its face and limbs incorporated the natural grain of the wood. Cuts were made in this wood, and then clothing made of silk crepe and gold brocade was pressed into the grooves. Because of this technique of inserting cloth into slits, these dolls were also called *kimekomi* dolls. Because they were made of willow wood, they were called *yanagi*, or "willow" dolls. The production of these dolls began in the Gembun era (1736-41), when Takahashi Tadashige, a caretaker at the Kamo Shrine, began using pieces of willow, left after the making of shrine utensils, to make dolls. It has been the traditional view that in the Bunka era (1804-18), Tadashige's grandson Daihachi was responsible for making these dolls popular. However, no records of Takahashi Tadashige can be found at the Kamo Shrine, and nowadays scholars take a negative view of this theory.

Regardless of the exact descent of Kamo dolls, it becomes apparent from the subjects they portray and the style of their garments that they were produced at the close of the Gembun era. Between the mid- to late-Edo period, many Kamo-*ningyô* dolls were produced.

With few exceptions, Kamo-*ningyô* dolls are usually small figures of 5-7 cm in length. There are even tiny Kamo dolls of less than a centimeter called *mame*-Kamo, or "bean-sized Kamo." It is as if these dolls live in a miniaturized world, brought to life by the incredibly fine technique of the craftsman. The particular hardness of willow wood allows for detailed carving, and allows the dolls, despite their minute proportions, to retain an elegant expression. Themes portrayed by Kamo dolls include: *hina* (no. 17), the Seven Gods of Good Fortune, Takasago—used as wedding ornaments for noblemen and commoners. Kamo-*ningyô* are the predecessors of present-day *kimekomi-ningyô*.

Fushimi-*ningyô*

Fushimi dolls were made of clay and sold in front of Kyoto's Fushimi-Inari Shrine. From ancient times, this area had produced pottery and these clay dolls began to be sold to shrine visitors as souvenirs. Their manufacture can be traced to before the Edo period. Specifically, it can be observed from *ukiyo-e* prints of the Genroku era, that dolls modeled on the image of Saigyô, a famous Buddhist

Sagara-*ningyô*: Daikoku; clay; ca. 1850-80, Yamagata prefecture

Hina-matsuri/Girls' Festival

No. 5, Plate Va; text, p. 29. Kamo-*ningyô*: Smiling Standing Figurine; ca. 1780-1800, Kyoto

Nos. 5, 6, 7/8, Plate Vb, text, p. 29. From left: Samurai with Retainer, No. 5. Sambasô; ca. 1780-1800, Kyoto

Fushimi-*ningyô*: Sumô Wrestler; clay, ca. 1850-80, Kyoto

Fushimi-*ningyô*: Oiran, ca. 1850-1880, Kyoto

Fushimi-*ningyô*: Dôji (Boy); clay, ca. 1850-80, Kyoto

master, were sold in front of the shrine.

In addition to Saigyô, various subjects such as Hotei, Manjukui, and Sumô wrestlers were represented by these dolls. Because they were shaped in wooden molds, the traditional shapes could be passed on to later generations. It is often remarked that Fushimi dolls have no backs. Indeed, it is one of their characteristics that neither design nor color is applied to their backs.

These earthen dolls gradually began to be produced in various locales. Perhaps the type which spread most widely was Manjukui, which means "sweet bean cake eater." This doll is based on the story of a young child, who, when asked whether he preferred his mother or father, broke one of these sweet bean cakes in half. He then turned to his questioner and asked, "Which part is more delicious?" The story became famous, and this type of doll was bought by parents who hoped that their children would be equally clever. In addition, at various locations, dolls made of earth or papier-mâché, modeled in the style of Fushimi dolls, were created. In this simple form is contained the prayers and hopes of common folk—a belief which has not changed throughout the ages.

Glossary

amagatsu: primitive ningyô type, together with hôko, see p. 11, no. 3
ayu: sweet fish
-bina: the word hina when used in combination with another word
buke: military nobility
cha-no-yu: tea ceremony
chadôgu: utensils for tea ceremony
chasen: bamboo whisk
chawan: tea bowl
chigowa: noble girl's hairstyle
Daikoku: god of wealth, one of the Seven Gods of Luck
dairi-bina: "Imperial couple" of the hina stand
denden taikô: children's toy
eboshi: headgear of samurai
eji/shichô: servants of hina stand
Friendship Doll: see no. 86
fur: see ke-ue-saiku
furisode-kimono: kimono with long sleeves
gempuku/kakan-no-gi: ceremony of attaining manhood
Genji-monogatari: see pp. 11, 12
Gion Festival: festival in Kyoto, 17th of July, with life-size figures on floats, see no. 35
go-gatsu yoroi-kazari: armor and weapon display of the Boys' Festival
go-gatsu-ningyô: figurine of the Boys' Festival
go-san-no-kiri: crest of Hideyoshi (see no. 34)
gofun: pulverized oyster shells mixed with rice paste or starch (see p. 29)
gonin-bayashi: five musicians of the hina stand
gosho-kuruma: Imperial carriage
gosho-ningyô: Imperial Palace ningyô, see pp. 19, 20, nos. 61-81
haiko: "crawling" baby
hariko: papier-mâché
harukoma: "spring horse," hobby horse, symbol of fertility
hina: "chicks," see p. 11
hina-byôbu: small screens behind the dairi-bina
hina-dan: tiered stand of display on Hina-matsuri
Hina-matsuri: Girls' Festival, March fifth, see p. 11
hina (-ningyô): figurine for the Girls' Festival
hishaku: bamboo laddle for tea ceremony
hôko: primitive ningyô type, together with amagatsu, see p. 11, no. 3
hoso-obi: narrow obi (girdle)
Ichimatsu-ningyô: play doll, originally portraying the actor Sanogawa Ichimatsu, see p. 21
iki-ningyô: life-size ningyô, see no. 85
inu-bako/inu-hariko: two boxes in shape of small dogs, see no. 4
ishô-fûzoku-ningyô: fashion-costume figurine
ishô-ningyô: costume figurine
jimmaku: battle screen
Jimmû Tennô: legendary first emperor of Japan
Jingû Kôgô/Takenouchi Sukune: legendary empress of Japan and her minister, see no. 35
jôba-gosho-ningyô: gosho-ningyô on horseback
kama: iron kettle of tea ceremony
kamishimo: type of dress, see no. 76
Kamo-ningyô: figurines made at Kamo shrine, see p. 22, nos. 5-8
karakuri-ningyô: mechanical ningyô figurines, see p. 22, nos. 65-67
kasuri: type of dress
katsuragae-ningyô: costume figurine with exchangeable wigs
kazari-uma: battle horse, displayed at Boys' Festival
ke-ue-saiku: technique to create fur with silk threads and paste, only in Kyoto

Glossary

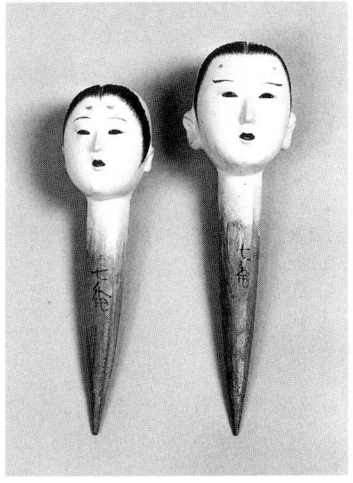 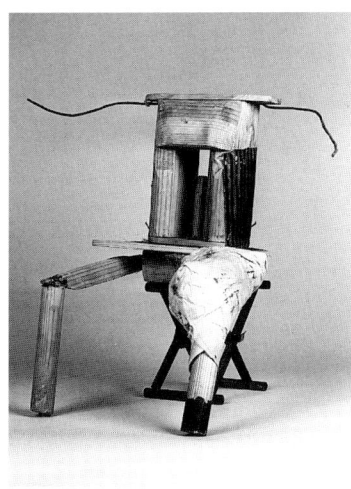

Hina-matsuri: Two Heads of *Hina* Figurines, ca. 1900, Kyoto; Inner Construction of Warrior Figurine

kensui: waste-water bowl in tea ceremony
kibori-kimekomi-bina: Girls' Festival figurines, carved from wood and dresses covered with textile, see no. 17
kin-no-tobi: bird of prey, a type of falcon, see nos. 36, 38
Kintoki/koitsuri-Kintoki: strong boy of Japanese legend, see no. 39
ko-tsuzumi: small hand drum of Nô orchestra
Kochô-no mai: children's dance of courtly Bugaku
kogata: small figurine
kokin-bina: Imperial couple in the kokin style, see p. 16, no. 16
kosode: kimono with short sleeves
kuge: court nobility, opposed to buke, see above
kuge-gyôretsu: carriage for a court noble, see p. 30, no. 26
kuro-mon-tsuki: type of dress of samurai class
Kyôho-bina: Imperial couple in the style of the Kyôho era, see p. 16, no. 11
mebina: female hina (empress), usual name used in Japan
mitate: parody of a Nô play, a Kabuki play, a hero or a mythological figurine
mitsu-ore: three-fold, type of doll which can sit in the Japanese way on its knees
mizu-hiki-de: hairstyle of gosho-ningyô, see p. 20, no. 75
mizura-gami: hairstyle of children in Heian period (9th to 12th c.)
mizusashi: cold-water container of tea ceremony
monigara: hulls
moriage: relief technique, see nos. 1, 2
musha-ningyô: figurine representing a warrior, displayed at Boys' Festival
naka-sori: hairstyle for small boys, see p. 80
ningyô: "human form," or "human shape," used in the catalogue as technical term for Japanese display dolls or figurines
Nô: classical Japanese theater using masks. The plays have a deep philosophical meaning
obina: male hina (emperor), usual name used in Japan, see mebina
ochôshi: sake container, carried by the ladies-in-waiting, no. 20
oiran: courtesan
onna-musha: female warrior, see no. 32
otogi-inu: fairytale dog, see inu-bako
ô-tsuzumi: large hand drum of Nô orchestra
Saga-ningyô: one of the oldest known types of ningyô, created in Saga, see p. 19, nos. 1, 2
Sambasô: auspicious Nô dance, New Year's performance
sambô: stand to offer sake cups, see no. 20
san'nin-kanjo: three ladies-in-waiting, court ladies who serve the Imperial couple, see no. 20
sandai-chigo: see no. 41, a young prince, presented for the first time to the emperor
sandai-ningyô/uizan: see no. 41
seikon-no-gi: Imperial wedding, see no. 56. Such figurines were created also on the occasion of the wedding of Emperor Akihito, as well as on the occasion of the wedding of the crown prince
sekko: plaster, used to produce ningyô, see p. 29
shishi-mai: lion dance, old dance with mythical lions, imported originally from China, dance on the occasion of the New Year's festivities
Shôki: the queller of demons, popular figurine of the Boys' Festival, see no. 40
Sumô: old wrestling sport of Japan
suô: dress of samurai
suwari-bina: "sitting hina," all types of seated dairi-bina, see p. 14, see hina
tachibina: standing hina figurine, see p. 14, nos. 9, 10
tachiko: standing child figurine
Taiko and Kiyomasa: see no. 34
taiko: drum beaten with drum sticks, Nô orchestra
Takasago: Nô play about an old couple, see no. 24/25
Takeda-ningyô: see p. 32, nos. 44-47
Tango-no-sekku: name of the Boys' Festival
Tengu: goblins of the wood, see no. 37
tennyo: fairy
tombo: lit. "dragonfly" hairstyle of small boys
tori-awase: cock-fighting at the Imperial court
tôso: modeling paste, made of sawdust and paste
tsukune: very small type of ningyô
uchikake: a kind of coat over the kimono
ukiyo-ningyô/ukiyo-mono: costume figurines with motifs of everyday life of the Edo period
Urade-yama: festival float of the Gion Festival, see no. 35
Urashima: legendary hero, see no. 35
utai: chant of Nô orchestra
waka-gimi/hime-gimi: young prince and young princess, gosho figurines dressed in the style of young nobles, see nos. 76, 77
yakko-mage: hairstyle of a commoner
yamabushi: itinerant mountain monks
Yanone: title of a famous Kabuki play
zuishin: guardian on the hina stand, see nos. 18, 19

Gosho-ningyô: *Karakuri-ningyô* with *Eboshi* Hat and Lion Mask; ca. 1850, Kyoto

No. 4, Plate VI; text, p. 29. *Hina-matsuri: Inu-bako*; papier-mâché, ca. 1900, Kyoto

Select Bibliography

WESTERN LANGUAGES:

Bassan, Pascale Chasseux. "Musha Ningyô: A Disappearing Samurai Heritage," *Arts of Asia* (March-April 1991), 124-133.

Baten, Lea. *The Image and the Motif: Japanese Dolls* (Tokyo, 1986).

Bottomley, Ian and Anthony Hopson. *Arms and Armor of the Samurai: The History of Weaponry in Ancient Japan* (New York, 1990).

Caiger, G. *Dolls on Display: Japan in Miniature* (Tokyo, 1933).

Gribbin, Jill and David. *Japanese Antique Dolls* (New York, Tokyo, 1984).

Japanese Dolls, Tourist Library, Vol. 17 (Tokyo, 1962).

Merthel, Timothy. "Japanese Samurai Dolls," *Circa: A Resource for the Connoisseur, Collector and Traveler* (Fall 1989), 20-27.

Schaarschmidt-Richter, Irmtraud. *Japanische Puppen (Japanese Dolls)* (Munich, 1962).

Society for the Development of International Cultural Relations (Kokusai Bunka Shinkôkai). *La Poupée Japonaise (The Japanese Doll)* (Tokyo, 1940).

Sue, Henny et al. *Karakuri Ningyô: An Exhibition of Ancient Festival Robots from Japan* (organized by The Japan Foundation and the Barbican Gallery) (London, 1986).

JAPANESE LANGUAGE:

Arisaka Kôtaro. *Nihon Gangu-shi* (1931).

———. *Hina-matsuri Shinkô* (1943).

Fujita Junko. *Hina to Hina no Monogatari* (Tokyo, 1993).

Ito Kaichi, ed. *Meihô Ningyô-shû* (Kyoto, 1937).

Kanemori Tokujiro. *Sekai Ningyô Meisakushû* (Kyoto, 1951).

Kawakami Shigeki. *Ningyô* (Kyoto National Museum exhibition catalogue) (Kyoto, 1993).

Kirihata Takeshi. *Gosho-ningyô*, Ningyô: Nihon to Sekai no Ningyô no Subete, Vol. 1 (Kyoto, 1985).

———. *Saga-ningyô, Kamo-ningyô, Ishô-ningyô*, Ningyô: Nihon to Sekai no Ningyô no Subete, Vol. 2 (Kyoto, 1985).

Kitamura Tetsurô. *Ningyô*, Nihon no Bijutsu, Vol. 11 (1967).

Kokuritsu Kokkai Toshokan. *Ningyô Bunkashiryô Tenrankai Mokuroku* (1949).

Omoya Shôzo. *Kyô Ningyô* (1976).

———. *Kyô Hina* (1982).

Ono Masao. *Hina to Hinadôgu* (Tokyo, 1979).

Saito Ryôsuke. *Hina Ningô to Musha Ningyô*, Ningyô: Nihon to Sekai no Ningyô no Subete, Vol. 4 (Kyoto, 1986).

———. *Gendai Nihon no Ningyô Sakka*, Ningyô: Nihon to Sekai no Ningyô no Subete, Vol. 5 (Kyoto, 1986).

Tawara Yûsaku. *Kyôdo Ningyô to Gangu*, Ningyô: Nihon to Sekai no Ningyô no Subete, Vol. 3 (Kyoto, 1986).

Yamada Tokubei. *Ningyô no Sekai*, Fureberu Shinsho, Vol. 16 (Tokyo, 1978 [2nd ed.]),

———. *Nihon Ningyô-shi* (Tokyo, 1984 [1991, 2nd ed.])
———. Sumie Kobayashi, ed., *Zusetsu Nihon no Ningyô-shi* (Tokyo, 1992).

Chronology

Nara	645-784	Edo	1615-1868
Heian	794-1185	Meiji	1868-1912
Kamakura	1185-1333	Taishô	1912-1926
Muromachi	1336-1568	Shôwa	1926-1989
Momoyama	1573-1615	Heisei	1989-

Miniature Birdcage

Photograph: courtesy of The Newark Museum

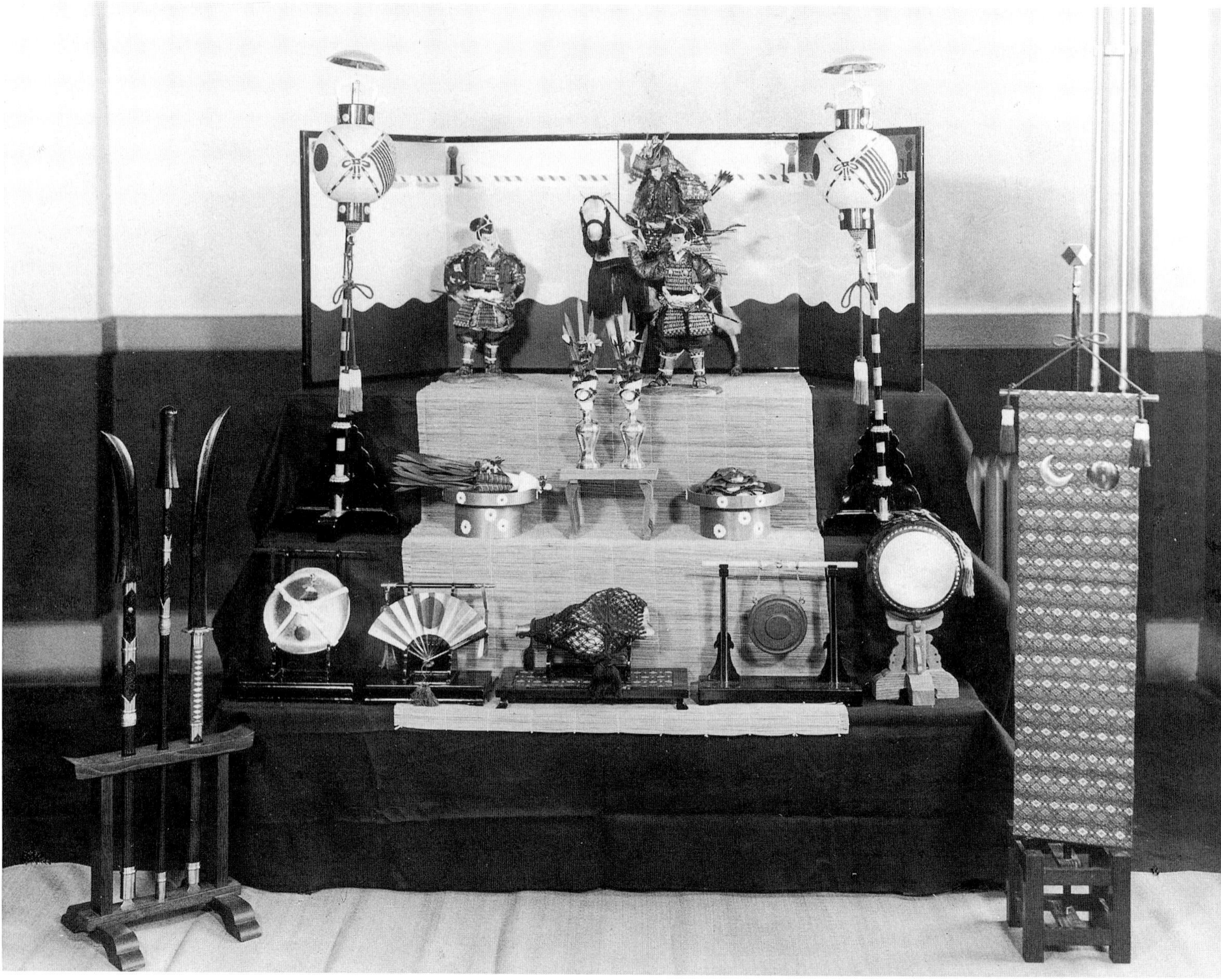

Boys' Festival; 1928, Kyoto, The Newark Museum

Entries

Sumie Kobayashi, Midori Aida and Kohichi Nakamura

Unless noted otherwise, all objects are from the Ayervais Collection.

TECHNICAL INFORMATION: Classical *hina-* and *go-gatsu-ningyô* were sometimes carved from wood and custom-made for the upper classes, while those for ordinary people were mass-produced using the *tôso* technique described in entry no. 71. This was true especially after the late Edo period. In either case, the heads and hands were covered with *gofun* (pulverized oyster shells mixed with rice paste). Now, most *ningyô* are produced by the *tôso* technique; masterpieces are carved in wood. The resulting products are characterized by their resistance to cracking and by their light weight. Masterpieces in this exhibition made by this technique are nos. 83 and 84. It is difficult to determine the material used simply by looking at the exterior of a figurine. Since 1970, *sekko* (plaster) has been utilized; but there are no examples in the Ayervais Collection. Heads and dressed bodies of *ishô-*, *hina-* and *go-gatsu-ningyô* were each created by different artisans. However, *ichimatsu-* and *gosho-ningyô* are still primarily the creations of individual dollmakers. Wood and sometimes straw were used for the bodies of *hina-* and *go-gatsu ningyô*. The stuffing in *ishô-ningyô* kimono could be cotton, straw, linen or hulls (*monigara*). Armor for *musha-ningyô* was primarily lacquered paper; in modern times metal has been used. Leather was solely for decorative purposes. Costumes of *hina* figurines are not lined. Large-size *gosho* figurines were usually carved from wood, while small ones were made primarily by the *tôso* technique. Papier-mâché was used especially for *karakuri-ningyô*.

Special Types of *Ningyô*

No. 1 (p. 6, plate I). SAGA-*NINGYO*: YOUNG BOY WITH SMALL DOG; early Edo period (ca. 1620); Saga; polychrome wood, gold and *moriage*; 25 cm. Here, the figurine depicts a smiling young boy carrying a little puppy under his arm. He sits cross-legged, his head still nodding, but the tongue (see no. 2) is inside of the head. His dress, with pigments and gold painted over a *gofun* ground, shows decorative elements that reflect the style of Buddhist sculpture of the time. Golden relief ornaments are created in a technique called *moriage*. (An ornament is first built up with *gofun*, then covered with gold powder diluted with paste). *Saga-ningyô* of this classical type are very rare and difficult to find in Western collections. This small sculpture is of excellent quality.

No. 2 (p. 18, plate IV). SAGA-*NINGYO*: YOUNG BOY WITH SMALL BIRD; early Edo period (ca. 1620); Saga; polychrome wood, gold and *moriage*; 16 cm; Peabody Essex Museum, Salem, MA, acc. no. E12514. This small figurine shows all the characteristics of *Saga-ningyô*: the head nods and, while doing so, a small tongue comes out of the mouth. This piece formerly belonged to the Ross Collection and was acquired by the museum in 1909.

No. 3 (p. 10, plate II). AMAGATSU AND HOKO; mid- to late-Edo period (ca.1780-1800); according to the owner: *amagatsu*: 17th c., *hôko*: 18th c.; Kyoto; *amagatsu*: 51 cm; *hôko*: 40 cm. These figurines can be called archetypes of Japanese *ningyô* and were used for purification rituals. Both are used to protect a newborn child from evil spirits. The existence of these *ningyô* is documented from the Heian period (8th-12th centuries, see p. 11). *Amagatsu* was a tradition in aristocratic (*kuge*) circles, while *hôko* was introduced to the world of commoners and later became a children's toy. Their function is similar to that of *inu-hariko* (no. 4, plate VI).

No. 4 (p. 26, plate VI). *INU-BAKO* ("DOG BOX") OR *INU-HARIKO*; mid-Meiji period (ca. 1900); Kyoto; height: 11 cm; width: 15 cm (each). These two *inu-bako* are made of papier-mâché with pigments, gold and *moriage*. *Inu-bako* are sometimes also called *otogi-inu* (fairytale dog). Along with *amagatsu* and *hôko*, they were used for the purification of newborn babies; in later periods, they were a trousseau item. During the mid-Edo period, small *inu-baku* were produced to be displayed on the *hina-dan*, the tiered stand for the *Hina-matsuri* (Girls' Festival). These two *inu-bako* were produced for such a stand; there, they should be placed so that they face each other.

Nos. 5, 6, 7/8 (p. 23, plates Va, b). KAMO-*NINGYO*; NO. 5: SMILING FIGURINE; NO. 6: SAMBASO DANCER; NO. 7/8: SAMURAI AND RETAINER; mid- to late-Edo period (ca. 1780-1800); Kyoto; no. 5: 7 cm; no. 6: 6 cm; no. 7/8: 7 cm. *Kamo-ningyo* are so-called because they were made at the Kamo Shrine. They were carved from the wood of willow trees. Utilizing a special technique, cloth was applied in the costume area. These types of figurines were the predecessors of present-day *kimekomi-ningyô* (see p. 22). Small in size, the smiling faces are characteristic of the type.

No. 9 (p. 15, plate IIIa). HINA-*NINGYO*: TACHIBINA; mid-Meiji period (ca.1900); Western Japan; male: 30 cm; female: 20 cm. These simple *ningyô* for the Girls' Festival were made in a rural area. A desire for good fortune is evident from the fortuitous symbols on the sleeves: a pine tree, blossoming plum and two elderly people from the Nô play, *Takasago* (see no. 24/25, p. 46). Made in a classical manner, these figurines cannot stand on their own, but must lean against a tier on the *hina* display stand.

No. 10 (p. 15, plate IIIb). HINA-*NINGYO*: TACHIBINA (STANDING HINA FIGURINES); early Meiji period (ca. 1880); Kyoto; *obina* ("emperor"): 30 cm; *mebina* ("empress"): 23 cm. These standing figurines remind us of the early style of *hina-ningyô*. Their dress is simple, with *kosode* and *hoso-obi* retaining the style of the Muromachi period (16th century). In the late Edo period, such figurines, in addition to the *dairi-bina* type (see nos. 11-17), were displayed as decoration on the *hina* stand. Differing from Edo-period *tachibina*, which cannot stand on their own, these figurines are made partially able to stand. Therefore, they probably were produced during the Meiji period.

Hina-matsuri/Girls' Festival

No. 11 (pp. 37 [detail], 38, 48 [detail]). KYOHO-BINA ("IMPERIAL COUPLE"); mid-Edo period (ca. 1750); Kyoto; *obina* ("emperor," with headgear): 79 cm; *mebina* ("empress," with crown): 74 cm. *Kyôho-bina* is a style of *hina-ningyô* for the Girls' Festival. They are called *Kyôho-bina* because the style has been popular since the Kyôho era (1716-35). Exceptionally unique and decorative, this style of dress is very different from that actually worn by court nobles (*kuge*). Because of its flamboyant quality, this kind of *hina* was preferred by common people who lived in urban areas. (The black of the mouth refers to a past custom of court aristocrats called *ohaguro*, which entailed dyeing the teeth black.)

No. 12a (p. 39, a). KYOHO-BINA; OBINA ("EMPEROR"); late Edo period (ca. 1800); from an unknown area (rural?); 22 cm. Because of the simple features, this *ningyô* probably belonged to ordinary people. Even though its features are similar to those on the female *hina* (no. 12 b), they are probably not a pair since the style and material of the costumes differ from each other. The heads might have been added afterwards. A comparison should be made between the dress of this *obina* and that of no. 13a. Incorrectly, this figurine was sold together with no. 12b under the assumption that they were an original pair. We purposely have combined them here to indicate the difficulty a Western collector might have in recognizing "matched" pieces.

No. 12b (p. 39, a). KOKIN-BINA, MEBINA ("EMPRESS"); late Edo period (ca.1830); Tokyo; 16 cm. The dress of this *mebina* should be compared with that of no. 16. This *hina* figurine was sold to accompany no. 12a. See above.

No. 13 (p. 39, b). DAIRI-BINA ("IMPERIAL COUPLE"); late Edo period (ca. 1820-30); Edo (Tokyo); *obina* ("emperor," with headgear): 23 cm; *mebina* ("empress"): 16 cm. These two figurines follow the style of the *Kyôho-bina*, but probably were made later, as indicated above. The crown does not belong to this *mebina*, but was sold to match the figurine. Therefore, it is displayed separately in the exhibition.

No. 14 (p. 40, a, b). HINA-DAN: GENJI-EMAKI HINA-BYOBU (PAIR OF MINIATURE FOLDING SCREENS WITH REPRESENTATIONS FROM THE TALE OF GENJI [GENJI-MONOGATARI]); late Edo period (ca. 1800); Kyoto; height: 29 cm; width: 72 cm (each). These folding screens depict scenes from this famous novel of the Heian period (ca. 1000). This type was frequently used for *hina* display. Clouds of a hexagon configuration, as depicted in the upper and lower areas, are very rare on a *hina-byôbu*.

No. 15 (p. 41). HINA-MATSURI: SMALL PALACE WITH EMPEROR AND EMPRESS; Kyoto; Meiji period (second half of 19th century); palace height: 56 cm; width: 49 cm; Peabody Essex Museum, Salem, MA, Balfour acc. no. 25737. This traditional, small hall contains only the figurines of an emperor and and empress in *kokin-bina* style, seated before a pair of golden screens. A bamboo shutter is rolled up, but could be let down to hide the illustrious couple. Red and black lacquer was used to decorate the building. Arranging *hina* figurines in a palacelike construction, rather than on a tiered stand, was popular in the old capital of Kyoto. An elaborate example of these palaces is exhibited in the Peabody Essex Museum.

No. 16 (p. 42, a, b). A PAIR OF KOKIN-BINA ("IMPERIAL COUPLE"); early Meiji period (ca. 1890); Kyoto; *obina* ("emperor," with headgear): 50 cm; *mebina* ("empress," with crown): ca. 49 cm. Very ornamental *kokin-bina* were created during the late Edo period in Edo (Tokyo); see page 16. As can be seen from the embroidery on the sleeves, the costume of this particular *mebina* goes beyond a realistic representation of a court costume. This pair was made in Kyoto and is an excellent representation of the *kokin-bina* style.

No. 17 (p. 43, a, b). KIBORI-KIMEKOMI-BINA (CARVED WOODEN HINA SET IN KIMEKOMI TECHNIQUE); late Meiji-early Taishô period (1910-20); place of origin unknown (Kyoto?); *dairi-bina*, *obina* (empress): 11 cm; platform: 6 cm. Although these *ningyô* look like Kamo-*ningyô*, they probably were produced by a wood carving artist as personal creative works. The set contains the "Imperial couple" (*dairi-bina*), the five musicians (*gonin-bayashi*) and two servants (*eji*). It is unknown if the figurines representing the three court ladies (*san'nin-kanjo*) and two guardians (*zuishin*) also existed. Rooster fighting (*tori-awase*) had long been held at the Imperial Palace on March 3, the day of the Girls' Festival; therefore, the two servants carry roosters.

No. 18 (p. 44, a). ZUISHIN (TWO GUARDIANS); late Edo period (ca. 1850); Tokyo, 26 cm. These guardians protect the court. They are dressed in the costumes of the Imperial guards of the Heian period, holding bows in their hands and arrows in a quiver on their backs. One is represented as an old, the other as a young, man.

No. 19 (p. 44, b). ZUISHIN (GUARDIAN, ONE FIGURINE); mid-Meiji period (late 19th century); Kansai area; 32 cm (with stand). This figurine of a guardian stands on a black lacquered pedestal. It might have been produced in a provincial area.

No. 20 (p. 44, c). SAN'NIN KANJO (THREE COURT LADIES); Taishô period (ca. 1920); Tokyo; standing figure: 18 cm. The three court ladies hold items for the feast. One carries a rice-wine (sake) container with a long handle, the other has one with a short handle; both vessels are called *ochôshi*. The seated figurine holds a small serving table (*sambô*) for sake cups.

No. 21/22 (p. 45 a, b). TWO FIGURINES FROM THE GONIN-BAYASHI (FIVE MUSICIANS); late Edo period (ca. 1830); Edo (Tokyo); no. 21: 17.5 cm; no. 22: 28 cm. Although the sizes are different, each is a figurine from the group of five musicians traditionally displayed together on a *hina* stand. In the late Edo period, this group was invented in Edo as an addition to those figurines already displayed on the tiered stand. They imitate musicians of the Nô orchestra, but have children's faces. Always very popular, these figurines bring a liveliness to the Girls' Festival display. The five boy musicians play Nô music in this sequence from right to left: the chant (*utai*), flute (*fue*), small hand drum (*ko-tsuzumi*), big hand drum (*ô-tsuzumi*), drum (*taikô*), see p. 8.

No. 23 (p. 45, c). EJI OR SHICHO (SERVANTS); late Edo period (ca 1850); Kyoto; standing: 21 cm, sitting 14 cm. These *hina* figurines, made in Kyoto, are considered to be servants of the court. They hold utilitarian objects: a broom, rake, bucket and ladle.

No. 24/25 (p. 46). ISHO-NINGYO FROM THE Nô PLAY, TAKASAGO; early Meiji period (ca. 1910); Kyoto; 27 cm (each). The figurines represent an elderly couple who are the protagonists of the famous Nô play, *Takasago*. They are popular because they celebrate long life. Therefore, they are often used to decorate the *hina* stand (see no. 9, plate VIa).

No. 26 (p. 46, a). HINA-DAN: KUGE-GYORETSU (PROCESSION CARRIAGE OF COURT ARISTOCRATS); early Meiji period (ca. 1880); Kyoto; carriage: (length) 100 cm x (depth) 29 cm x (height) 43 cm. This ensemble represents the Imperial Palace carriage (*gosho-guruma*) drawn by an ox and accompanied by several retainers. Shown is the ox boy, a retainer, and three servants carrying shoes, an umbrella and headgear. A small bench facilitates getting out of the carriage, and serves to keep it in position when the ox is unhitched. From the crest on the carriage, we can judge that it was made as part of a noble family's *hina* set. The ox was made by the *ke-ue saiku* technique (see no. 30), used exclusively in Kyoto.

No. 27 (p. 47, b). ISHO-NINGYO: KOCHO-NO-MAI (COSTUME FIGURINE: BUTTERFLY DANCE); Meiji period (ca. 1880); Kyoto, 23 cm (each). As the number of tiers on the *hina* stand gradually increased during the 19th century, the types of display figurines also increased; flamboyant types became especially popular. These figurines are a kind of *ishô-ningyô*, also called *ukiyo-ningyô* or *ukiyo-mono* (*ningyô* of the Floating World), because they represent various genre scenes. Here, two boys with attached butterfly wings perform a famous dance of Bugaku (Heian-period court dances, 9th-12th centuries). It was traditionally performed by children and is mentioned in *The Tale of Genji* (*Genji-monogatari*). Hina-*ningyô* are sometimes imaginative and do not precisely copy original representations. These two figurines are of excellent quality.

No. 28 (pp. 49 [detail], 51). MUSHA-NINGYO (WARRIOR); mid-Edo period (ca. 1750); Kyoto; warrior: 56 cm; attendant: 36 cm. Figurines such as these two frequently have been displayed on May 5, the Boys' Festival (*Tango-no-sekku*). Special features of this kind of *ningyô* produced in Kyoto are fair complexions and calm expressions. This warrior could not be identified. According to the collector, this figurine probably represents Yoshitsune.

No. 29 (p. 50, b). GO-GATSU YOROI-KAZARI (ARMOR DECORATION OF THE BOYS' FESTIVAL); Taishô period (ca. 1920); Tokyo; screen width: 133 cm. In the center of the display for the Boys' Festival (*Tango-no-sekku* or *Go-gatsu-matsuri*) is a set of arms, armor and other warlord paraphernalia, displayed in front of a miniature battle screen (*jimmaku*). The whole arrangement imitates a medieval exhibit of battle arms belonging to a warlord. On the helmet, the large dragonfly symbolizes male bravery.

No. 30 (p. 50, a). KAZARI-UMA (DECORATED BATTLE HORSE); Meiji period (ca. 1900); Kyoto; 42 cm x 42 cm. This handsomely adorned military horse is displayed on the Boys' Festival stand. Its hairy body is produced by a technique called *ke-ue-saiku* ("fine work of fur planting"), in which silk yarn is pasted on.

No. 31 (p. 52). MUSHA-NINGYO (WARRIOR); mid-Edo period (ca. 1740); Kyoto; 35 cm. This warrior cannot be identified. Using actual human hair for the hairstyle is very rare for this type of *ningyô*. Except for nos. 1 and 2 published here in the catalogue, this is the oldest example of *ningyô* in the exhibition.

No. 32 (p. 53, b). MUSHA-NINGYO (ONNA-MUSHA: FEMALE WARRIOR?); mid- to late-Edo period (ca. 1800); Kyoto; 37 cm. The figurine is adorned with the hairstyle of a woman. Stories about women who wore men's clothes and fought in battles are known from the *Tales of the Gempei Battles* (1159-85) waged between the Taira and the Minamoto clans; but it has not been possible to identify this *onna-musha* as one of the known female heroines of the time. The spear she holds might have been added later.

No. 33 (p. 53, a). MUSHA-NINGYO (YOUNG WARRIOR); Meiji period (ca. 1900); Tokyo; 31 cm. This *ningyô* represents the figure of a warrior on a battlefield. His hair is untied in order to be able to wear a helmet. The figurine cannot be identified. Its flesh-colored face is characteristic of *ningyô* made in Tokyo during this period.

No. 34 (p. 54). MUSHA-NINGYO: TAIKO AND KIYOMASA (WARRIOR FIGURINES: TOYOTOMI HIDEYOSHI [1535-1598] AND HIS RETAINER, KATO KIYOMASA [1562-1611]); 1780-1800; Kyoto; Hideyoshi: 37 cm, retainer: 31cm. The main figure might be identified as Taikô (Toyotomi Hideyoshi) because he wears a golden Chinese-style cap and the family crest of *Go-san-no-Kiri* (five and three paulownia leaves). Katô Kiyomasa, who accompanied Hideyoshi on his campaign against Korea and was famous for his bravery, is probably the warrior holding Taikô's spear.

No. 35 (p. 55). MUSHA-NINGYO: JINGU KOGO (EMPRESS JINGU); mid-Edo period (ca. 1780); Kyoto; empress: 56 cm (with cap); Takenouchi Sukune: 40 cm; attendant: 35 cm. Empress Jingû was a legendary ruler (traditional chronology: AD 170-269). According to ancient legend, she gave birth on the battlefield to the prince who would become the Emperor Ojin (traditional chronology: 201-310), while hiding the fact of the death of her husband, the Emperor Chuai. She is a very popular figurine among those displayed for the Boys' Festival. Next to her an old warrior, her faithful minister Takenouchi Sukune—considered to be the Japanese Methusalah—keeps the newborn infant in his arms; a lower-ranking attendant holds a banner. In this representation, Empress Jingû fishes for *ayu* (sweet fish) with her bow, in a scene based upon an episode in which she had been able to divine by this same means the outcome of the war against Korea. The same representation appears in the *urade-yama* (festival car), a float with larger-than-life size figures in Kyoto's Gion Festival. In her other hand, the empress holds a commander's fan.

No. 36 (p. 56). MUSHA-NINGYO: JIMMU TENNO (EMPEROR JIMMU); mid-Meiji period (ca. 1900); Tokyo; 30 cm (see also no. 38). The costume and accessories on this figurine are probably rare. Emperor Jimmu usually holds a bow; here, what looks like a stick is in reality half of his bow. The top part, where the golden kite (*kin-no-tobi*; a type of hawk) usually sits, is missing.

No. 37 (p. 57). TENGU KING (KING OF LONG-NOSED GOBLINS IN THE WOODS); late Edo-early Meiji period (ca. 1850-80); Tokyo; 31 cm. *Tengu* (goblins) are believed to live in a magical world. Higher-class long-nosed *tengu* are mischievous. Lower-class *tengu* have wings or the features of a bird, including a beak. They serve human-looking *tengu*. All are dressed like itinerant mountain monks (*yamabushi*). The *tengu* king represented here has a red face with big eyes and a very long, up-turned nose. With the feather fan he holds in his hand, he is capable of flying through the sky. This kind of *ningyô* very often is represented in a scene together with the young Minamoto Yoshitsune, the handsome hero of the 12th-century battle tales of Gempei. The *tengu* king taught him the art of Japanese fencing at Mount Kurama near Kyoto. During that time, Yoshitsune still carried his childhood name, Ushiwakamaru. They are often displayed together at the Boys' Festival.

No. 38 (p. 58). MUSHA-NINGYO: JIMMU TENNO (EMPEROR JIMMU); mid-Meiji period (ca. 1890); Tokyo; 41 cm. Jimmu was a legendary emperor who was said to have been the first to hold this position in Japan. This representation is based on the myth that he subjugated enemies with the help of a golden bird of prey, a member of the hawk family called a kite (Jpn.: *kin-no-tobi*; Latin: *milvus*), which flew down from heaven on the tip of his bow. This *ningyô* was invented after the Meiji Restoration of 1868.

No. 39 (p. 59, a). KOITSURI-KINTOKI (KINTOKI, THE STRONG BOY, FISHING FOR A CARP); early Showa period (ca. 1930-40); Tokyo; 28 cm (including platform). This *ningyô* represents Kintoki (or Kintarô) catching an enormous carp. Kintoki was a strong, healthy boy who, according to legend, lived in the wilds of Mt. Ashigara. This is a very popular figurine for the Boys' Festival. The carp is also important for that holiday, as the symbol of diligent studies and the ability to overcome life's difficulties. In the 1930s, a whole series of representations of Kintarô were created, depicting the legendary strong boy engaged in many activites.

No. 40 (p. 59, b). SHOKI (CH'UNG KUEI); mid-Meiji period (ca. 1900); Tokyo; 45 cm. According to Chinese legend, the emperor of the T'ang dynasty, Ming-huang (Gensô; reigned: 712-56), was tormented in his dreams by an evil demon. A hero named Ch'ung Kuei appeared to him and tortured the demon. Ch'ung Kuei was in reality a young scholar who had successfully passed the Imperial examinations; but when he presented himself before Ming-huang, the emperor was terrified because he was so unsightly. Distraught by the emperor's reaction, the young man committed suicide, and subsequently was deified as the famous queller of demons. Shôki, as he was called in Japan, was adopted for the Boys' Festival as a deity to expel demons. Numerous versions of this story exist. This type of *ningyô* is employed primarily in Tokyo and vicinity.

No. 41 (p. 60). SANDAI-NINGYO (COURT-VISITING NINGYO) OR UIZAN ("FIRST VISIT"); late Edo period (ca. 1800); Kyoto; 13 cm. This *ningyô* is also called *sandai-chigo* (court-visiting child). It was given by the emperor, as a commemorative gift of greeting, to a prince on his first visit to the Imperial Palace. The costume is customary daily dress for children of the court aristocracy (*kuge*). This is an extraordinarily rare type of *ningyô*.

No. 42 (p. 61, a). SMALL BOY; late Edo period (ca. 1820); Edo (Tokyo); 7 cm; Peabody Essex Museum, Salem, MA, Balfour acc. no. 25737. This small figurine of a boy might have been one of the musicians associated with the Girls' Festival *hina* display stand (see nos. 21 and 22). His face shows the characteristics of the much older Jirozaemon-style *ningyô* (see p. 16). Dressed in blue and gold brocade, he wears a kimono with orange silk sleeves embroidered with gold threads.

No. 43 (p. 61, b). GEMPUKU (KAKAN-NO-GI) (CEREMONY OF ATTAINING MANHOOD [OR CEREMONY OF CROWNING]); late Edo period (ca. 1780); Kyoto; center: 38 cm; right (brown): 38 cm; left (blue): 33 cm. These three figurines are dressed in *suô* kimono and *eboshi* caps, a ceremonial costume for middle-class samurai. Only the central *ningyô*, who holds a red lacquered cup with a stand in front, represents a young man. Therefore, the figurines illustrate the ritual of *gempuku*, the ceremony celebrating a boy's attainment of manhood. The samurai on the left and right are assumed to be his valued, personal assistants. This ritual was also called the "Ceremony of Crowning." Wearing a cap and shaving the forelock (from the 16th century on) were very important components in this coming-of-age ceremony observed from the 7th century through the Edo period. Normally, it took place between the ages of ten and fifteen, after a boy had reached the height of 136 cm (4.5 ft.). This type of *ningyô* is very difficult to find, even in Japan.

No. 44 (p. 62). TAKEDA-STYLE ONNA-NINGYO: MITATE ONNA-URASHIMA (TAKEDA-STYLE FEMALE NINGYO: PARODY OF FEMALE URASHIMA); late Edo period (ca. 1850); Kyoto; 35.5 cm; with stand: 40 cm. This figurine might be a type of Takeda-*ningyô*. At the same time, it has the beauty of an *ishô-ningyô* of high quality. Usually Urashima is represented as a man holding a fishing rod; therefore, the bow and arrow could have been added later. The story of Urashima tells of a young man taken by a turtle to the bottom of the sea, where he married the delightful princess Otohime, daughter of the Dragon King of the Sea. When he finally returned to earth, he had spent three hundred years under the ocean. After breaking his promise not to open the box given to him by the princess, Urashima could never go back to the Dragon King's domain. He instantly became old and died. This is a very popular fairy tale in Japan. The figurine presented here might be a parody (*mitate*) of this story.

No. 45 (p. 63, a). TAKEDA-NINGYO (TITLE UNKNOWN); late Edo period (ca. 1800); Kyoto; 37 cm. Takeda-*ningyô* which imitated mechanical dolls of the Takeda Theater in Osaka were sold as souvenirs. Nevertheless, this kind of *ningyô* was produced in Kyoto. (However, it is still unclear if this *ningyô* really represents a Takeda *ningyô* because they usually were placed on a boxlike stand). We assume this figurine represents Oboshi Yaranosuke, a character from the Kabuki play, *Chûshingura* (The Treasury of Loyal Retainers). The character pretends to be a drunkard, in order to deceive his enemies and successfully revenge his master's death.

No. 46 (p. 63, b). TAKEDA-NINGYO (TITLE UNKNOWN); late Edo period (ca. 1850); Kyoto; 35 cm. The figurine is dressed like a traveling monk (*rokubu*). Features of Takeda *ningyô* can be seen in its exaggerated expression and pose. (See p. 21)

No. 47a, b (p. 64). TAKEDA-NINGYO (TWO FIGHTING HEROES); late Edo period (ca. 1830); Kyoto; a) 80 cm (total height with stand), figurine: 63 cm (with headgear); b) 97 cm (total height with banner), figurine: 61 cm (with headgear), stand: 17 cm. At the time when these two figurines were created, Takeda-*ningyô* were made in Kyoto, but sold in Osaka. Takeda-*za*, a puppet theater in business since 1662, which presented only mechanical *ningyô*, was very popular in Osaka. Based on puppets, figurines such as these were made as souvenirs. Exaggerated expressions and poses are characteristic. The stands for these figurines are unique. These *ningyô* wear robes embroidered with dragons and tigers: the breath of the latter symbolizes the wind, while that of the dragon represents water—two of the most powerful elements. These figurines might have been created as a pair which take their themes from stories of brave warriors.

No. 48 (p. 65). MITSU-ORE: SUMO-NINGYO (COSTUME FIGURINE: SUMO WRESTLER); early Meiji period (ca. 1860-80); Kyoto; 25 cm. This figurine depicts a Sumô wrestler entering the ring. Sumô was very popular as a national sport in Japan when this *ningyô* was made, and it might represent a popular wrestler of the time. It is a three-fold *ningyô* made of papier-mâché (*hariko*). Boys of the nobility during the Heian period played with dolls in the shape of Sumô wrestlers.

No. 49 (p. 66). CHA-NO-YU (TEA CEREMONY); mid-Meiji period (ca. 1900); Kyoto; 20 cm. The figurine represents a tea master practising the tea ceremony. A kettle (*kama*) to heat water stands on a brazier. In front of the figurine are the necessary tea utensils (*chadôgu*): the fresh-water jar (*mizusashi*), tea caddy (*chaire*), bamboo whisk (*chasen*), bamboo laddle (*hishaku*), waste-water bowl (*kensui*), and black raku-ware tea bowl (*chawan*). Some minor objects are missing in the exhibition; the tea bowl is not in the photograph in the catalogue.

No. 50 (p. 67). SAMBASO (SAMBASO DANCER); late Edo period (ca. 1850); Edo (Tokyo); 33 cm. This childlike figurine, which should hold bells in one hand, dances Sambasô—the most auspicious work in the Nô theater, performed to celebrate the New Year. The dance-play was also introduced into Kabuki, where it is performed with the same characteristics. Sambasô in a Nô play wears the black mask of an old man. The figurine is presented here with a golden ball; his original accessory (bells) was found after the photograph in this catalogue was taken.

No. 51 (p. 68). ISHO FUZOKU NINGYO (COSTUME-GENRE FIGURINE); mid-Edo period (ca. 1780); Kyoto; 26 cm. This *ningyô* wears the fashionable attire of a young woman in the mid-Edo period. Her hair is coiled up in a bun, affixed with a pin. She wears at least four different kimono one above the other—the last having a yellow-and-red checked design. These layers are held together by a large red brocade obi. On top of this outfit she wears a long, narrow *uchikake* coat with a floral medallion design and red lining. This is an excellent example of a fashion doll produced during the Edo period.

No. 52 (p. 69, b). MITSU-ORE JOSEI FUZOKU NINGYO (THREE-FOLD FEMALE GENRE OR FASHION NINGYO); late Edo period (ca. 1790); Kyoto; 35 cm. This figurine of a woman was created as a fashion *ningyô* of its time. It wears an embroidered kimono, and a change of apparel hangs on the traditional black-lacquer kimono stand. This figurine might have been a play doll for children of the upper classes.

No. 53 (p. 69, a). JOSEI GASSO SUGATA (WOMEN MUSICIANS); late Edo period (ca. 1800); Edo (Tokyo); left and right: 28 cm; center: 25 cm. In the center, a woman plays the koto, the thirteen-string, half-tube, plucked zither that is one of the oldest instruments of

Japan. On each side sit other women playing the shamisen, the three-string plucked lute. These *ningyô* represent the customs of Edo.

No. 54 (p. 70). MODEL OF A LANTERN SHOP; width: 50 cm; Meiji period (ca. 1900); Tokyo; Peabody Essex Museum, Salem, MA, acc. no. E8539; Billings Fund, 1906. This small model belongs to a series of shop models owned by the Peabody Essex Museum. These include: a hardware store, porcelain store and ribbon shop. They were created in Japan primarily to fill orders placed by Westerners and became very popular in Western ethnographical museums of the time. Lanterns for various businesses are for sale, including: one with the characters "Yoshiwara," the traditional pleasure quarter in Edo (Tokyo); two with the American flag; two others with the characters *"Dai Nihon Banzai"* (Great Japan, Hurrah!); and another with the characters *"hônô"* (offering). A woman dressed as a merchant's wife is sitting on the tatami floor.

No. 55 (p. 71, a, b). KATSURAGAE-NINGYO (WIG-CHANGING FIGURINE); mid-Meiji period (ca. 1900); Kyoto; 23 cm. This charming fashion *ningyô* possesses a variety of hairstyles that can be achieved by changing its wigs. It has thirty-two of them, each with a different name. The *ningyô* is a *mitsu-ore* type.

No. 56 (p. 72, a, b). SEIKON-NO-GI (IMPERIAL WEDDING); Taishô period, probably 1924; Kyoto; male: 42 cm; female: 40 cm. These figurines are probably wearing replicas of costumes worn at the wedding of the future Shôwa Emperor (1901-1989), who married Princess Nagako (born 1903) in 1924.

No. 57 (p. 73, a). MODERN ISHO-NINGYO (COSTUME FIGURINE: BEAUTIFUL WOMAN); after 1945; from unknown area; 35 cm. This figurine, made by a contemporary craftsperson, cannot be called an *ishô-ningyô* in the real sense because it is impossible to identify it with any fashion or genre-type *ningyô* of the pre-Meiji period. The craftsperson may have obtained inspiration from 19th-century *ukiyo-e* prints and interpreted these models rather freely. This kind of *ningyô*—also beautifully made—should not be called genuine *ishô-ningyô*, but is attractive, nonetheless.

No. 58 (p. 73, c). OIRAN (COURTESAN OF EDO PERIOD); 1955, Osaka; 55 cm; Museum of the City of New York, acc. no. 55.40 a-d; Gift of the Mayor of New York City. This costume *ningyô* was presented in 1955 to Robert Wagner, Mayor of New York City from 1954 to 1965, by the Osaka Steamship Company (Osaka Shosen Kaisha) on the one-hundredth anniversary of Commodore Perry's opening of Japan to world commerce. It represents the old Japanese tradition of presenting a doll as an auspicious gift. The figurine depicts a courtesan created by a modern craftsperson inspired by 19th-century *ukiyo-e* prints.

No. 59 (p. 73, b). HAGOROMO ("THE FEATHER ROBE"); Shôwa period (1960); Kansai region; 26 cm. This figurine represents a dancing fairy (*tennyo*) from the Nô play, *Hagoromo*. It is an excellent example of contemporary *ningyô*.

No. 60 (p. 74). MIZURA-GAMI (MIZURA HAIRSTYLE); early Meiji period (ca. 1880); Kyoto; 35 cm. By utilizing the head of a *gosho-ningyô*-style figurine, this represents a boy of the Heian period (9th-12th centuries). The hair style, called *mizura*, was used at that time for children.

Gosho-ningyô/Imperial Palace Figurines

No. 61 (pp. 75 [detail], 76, 77, b). GOSHO-NINGYO (UNTITLED); late Edo period (ca. 1780); Kyoto; 28 cm. Judging from the pose, this *ningyô* was probably originally depicted as dragging an object.

Presumably it dates from a relatively early period for *gosho-ningyô*. The kimono was made later to fit the figurine in this particular pose.

No. 62 (p. 77, a) GOSHO-NINGYO (UNTITLED); late Edo period (ca. 1830); Kyoto; 29 cm. This figurine, like no. 63, is a typical example of a *gosho-ningyô*. It implies dynamic motion.

No. 63 (p. 78). HARUKOMA MOCHI (SPRING HORSE HOLDER); late Edo period (ca.1830); Kyoto; 46 cm (with the hobby horse). Frequently *gosho-ningyô* hold various toys which have auspicious meanings. This one holds a hobby horse, symbolizing fertility, in celebration of the New Year.

No. 64 (p. 79, a). DAIKOKU-MITATE; mid-Meiji period (ca. 1880-90); Kyoto; 21 cm. With a bale of rice lying at his side and a golden sake cup in his hand, this figurine is a parody of the God of Wealth, Daikoku, one of the Seven Gods of Good Fortune. *Gosho-ningyô* often represent this type of folk figure. Stylistically, the figurine resembles more popular *gosho-ningyô*, such as nos. 69-71.

No. 65 (p. 79, b). KARAKURI GOSHO-NINGYO: HARUKOMA MOCHI (MECHANICAL GOSHO-NINGYO: SPRING HORSE HOLDER); late Edo period (ca. 1830); Kyoto; 23 cm. This *gosho-ningyô* has hands that can be moved up and down, due to a mechanism built into its back.

No. 66 (p. 80). KARAKURI GOSHO-NINGYO: MITATE-SHISHI-MAI (MECHANICAL GOSHO-NINGYO: PARODY OF A LION DANCE); 19th century; Kyoto; 37 cm. This mechanical *ningyô* has arms that can be lifted up and down. It parodies a lion dance. On its head is a hat in the shape of a red peony. The decorative cushion on which it sits did not belong originally to this figurine.

No. 67 (p. 81). KARAKURI GOSHO-NINGYO: DENDEN TAIKO (BOY WITH EBOSHI HAT AND DENDEN DRUM [TAIKO]); 19th century; Kyoto; 30 cm. This mechanical *ningyô* has arms that can be elevated. It holds a traditional toy.

No. 68 (p. 82). JOBA-GOSHO-NINGYO (FIGURE OF A CHILD ON HORSEBACK); late Edo period (ca. 1840); Kyoto; 32 cm. This represents the figure of a young boy from a warrior family (*buke*) riding. On its head is a woven, lacquered battle hat. The horse was produced by using the *ke-ue saiku* technique, developed exclusively in Kyoto (see nos. 26 and 30).

Nos. 69, 70, 71 (p. 83, c). No. 69: DENDEN-DAIKO MOCHI (DRUM HOLDER); No. 70: HAIHAI-NINGYO (CRAWLING NINGYO); No. 71: TAIKO-TATAKI (DRUMMER); late Edo period (all ca. 1850); Kansai area; no. 69: 19 cm; no. 70: 12 cm; no. 71: 30 cm. It can be assumed that these popular *gosho-ningyô* were made in the Kansai area as souvenirs. Their bodies are made of *hariko* (papier-mâché) and *tôso*. The latter is a technique used for mass production, in which paulownia sawdust mixed with paste is made into a claylike modeling material that can be used in molds.

No. 72 (p. 83, b). YAKKO-MAGE ("COMMONER'S TOPKNOT"); late Edo period (ca. 1830); Kyoto; 5.5 cm. This small figurine belongs to the *tsukune* type of *gosho-ningyô* which were kneaded and rounded by hand. (*Tsukuneru* means to knead and make round). They often depict the charming gestures of small children. This figurine has a commoner's hairstyle, which is very rare in this type of *ningyô*. The pedestal did not originally belong to this figurine.

Gosho-ningyô/Imperial Palace Figurines— Ichimatsu-ningyô/Iki-ningyô

No. 73 (p. 83, a). HAIKO (CRAWLING BABY); mid-Meiji period (ca. 1900); Kyoto; 19 cm. This *ningyô*, imitating real *gosho-ningyô*, was made for ordinary people.

No. 74 (p. 84). MITATE-NO-NINGYO (TWO FIGURINES AS A PARODY OF A NÔ PLAY); late Edo period (ca.1830); Kyoto; 33 cm (each). *Mitate* means to compare to (or to parody) the protagonist of a narrative play. These *ningyô* might be associated with a Nô drama. Judging from their costumes, the play might have taken its theme from a Chinese anecdote. The red *hakama* on the lefthand *ningyô* might have been added later. A helmet belonging to the righthand figurine was found after the photograph in this catalogue was taken.

No. 75 (p. 85). MITATE-YANONE (PARODY OF THE ARROWHEAD); late Edo period (ca. 1800-50); Kyoto; 35 cm. Judging from the large arrow in its hand, this figurine might represent a parody of the famous Kabuki play, *Yanone*, first staged by the famous actor, Ichikawa Danjurô I, in 1729. The play's theme is related to dramas based on the Soga brothers' revenge. Painted on the head of the figurine is a pattern known as "*mizu-hiki-de*" along with carefully delineated strands of hair.

No. 76 (p. 86). WAKA-GIMI-HIME-GIMI (BOY AND GIRL FROM A NOBLE FAMILY); late Edo period (ca. 1820); Kyoto; 47 cm (each). These two figurines represent a boy and girl from an upper-class samurai family (*buke*). The boy wears a black kimono with crest (*kuro-mon-tsuki*) and ceremonial apparel known as *kamishimo*. With hair tied in the *chigowa* manner—typical for young, upper-class girls—the female figurine is clothed in an *uchikake* (coat) over a kimono.

No. 77 (p. 87, a, b). MITSU-ORE GOSHO NINGYO: WAKAGIMI-HIMEGIMI (THREE-FOLD PALACE NINGYO: A BOY AND GIRL FROM A NOBLE FAMILY); late Edo period (ca. 1850); Kyoto; 30 cm (each). These *ningyô* are dressed in ceremonial costumes appropriate for children of the samurai class (*buke*). They might have been commissioned by a *daimyô* (feudal lord) family. Real human hair is rarely utilized for the hairstyles of *gosho-ningyô*.

No. 78 (p. 88, a). KOGATA MITSU-ORE GOSHO-NINGYO (SMALL THREE-FOLD PALACE NINGYO); late Edo period (ca. 1800); Kyoto; 15 cm. "Three-fold" (*mitsu-ore*) is the technical term for dolls which could be made to sit down with their legs folded under them. This type of *gosho-ningyô* may have functioned as play dolls for children of the upper classes. The costume with its detailed embroidery seems to have been made especially for this doll. A purse with fringe is attached to its girdle.

No. 79 (p. 88, b). KUGE-TACHIKO (STANDING CHILDREN OF COURT ARISTOCRATS); Meiji to Taishô period (ca. 1900-20); Kyoto; 18 cm (each). This is a pair of male and female *ningyô*—dressed as children of the *kuge* nobility.

No. 80 (p. 89, a). KOGATA-GOSHO-NINGYO; late Edo period (ca. 1840-50); Kyoto; 10 cm. Even though this doll is one of the standing *gosho-ningyô* called *tachiko*, it is made much smaller than the usual *tachiko-ningyô*. Because of its costume, it must have been a play doll. Its *naka-sori* hairstyle, shaved only in the middle of the head, is a common one for children between the ages of three and five.

No. 81 (p. 89, b). TACHIKO (STANDING CHILD IN COMMONER'S DRESS); late Edo period (ca. 1850); Kyoto; 27 cm. This *gosho-ningyô* is able to stand. It might have been used as a play doll.

Ichimatsu-ningyô/Iki-ningyô

No. 82 (p. 90, a). URBAN COMMONER'S CHILD; Tempô era, late Edo period (ca. 1840); Kyoto; 47 cm. This *ningyô* is a play doll, dressed in the garb of an urban commoner's child. The legs are three-fold (*mitsu-ore*). It wears a tea-brown and black striped kimono with a green obi. An additional white *furisode*-kimono was made for it in modern times. A box created especially for this doll carries the inscription of Nishizawa Tekiho (see p. 7), with a dedication to the well-known American doll collector, Eloise M. Thomas.

No. 83 (p. 90, b). LITTLE BOY; Meiji-Taisho period (ca.1900-20); Tokyo; 60 cm. Characteristic of this Ichimatsu-*ningyô* made in Tokyo are a naturalistic facial expression and utilization of flesh-colored pigments. The costume is that of an ordinary child during Meiji-Taishô times. It wears a brown and black kimono, woven in *kasuri* technique, with a purple obi and attached small purse.

No. 84 (p. 91). LITTLE BOY WITH TOMBO HAIR STYLE; mid-Meiji period (ca. 1900); Tokyo; 33 cm. This depiction of a little boy is clothed in the dress worn by ordinary children during the time. Its hairstyle is called *tombo* (dragonfly).

No. 85 (p. 92). IKI-NINGYO (LIFE-SIZE FIGURINE: PEASANT MOTHER CARRYING BABY ON HER BACK); Meiji period (ca. 1880); Tokyo; 140 cm (height of the mother); Peabody Essex Museum, Salem, MA, acc. no. E16310; Morse Collection. Edward Sylvester Morse (1838-1925) brought back from Japan a group of life-size figurines representing different classes of Japanese families. They are striking because of their lifelike appearance. Such figurines were exceptionally popular in the West for ethnographical collections. In Japan, they were used as drapers' models until the Taishô period when Western-style mannequins were introduced.

No. 86a, b, c (p. 93, a, b). FRIENDSHIP DOLLS (ICHIMATSU-*NINGYO*)
a) MISS OSAKA; 1928; The Newark Museum, acc. no. 28.966; 83.8cm
b) YOUNGER BROTHER; 1928; acc. no. 28.967; 53.3 cm; both a Gift of the Committee on World Friendship Among Children, 1928
c) YOUNGER SISTER; 1989; acc. no. 90.486; Gift of the City of Osaka, 1990; made by Shokensai Toko II
In 1926, 12,379 dolls, called "blue-eyed messengers" were sent to Japan as a gesture of good will between the two countries. The following year, the Japanese responded and sent 58 exquisite friendship dolls (Ichimatsu or Yamato-*ningyô*), made by the most famous *ningyô* makers of the time, to the United States. During World War II, many of the American dolls were destroyed in Japan, often ritually burned as symbols of the enemy. To date, around four hundred have survived. In the United States twenty-three figurines have been lost, some because of similar hostile attitudes, while thirty-five have been located in libraries and museums all over the United States. Donald Richie wrote an article on the American "messengers" in Japan, published in the June 1982 *Japan Society Newsletter*; a year later, the Japanese designer Kei Kobayashi investigated the fate of the Japanese "messengers" in the United States. Valrae Reynolds, curator of Asian art at The Newark Museum, described the fate of the "black-eyed messengers" in an article in the September 1983 *Japan Society Newsletter*. Miss Osaka traveled to the United States with an elaborate trousseau, which has been completely preserved. It includes: musical instruments (shamisen and hand drum); everyday and formal tea sets; her visiting card; and even her cookies. Letters from Japanese school girls accompanied her, revealing the Japanese belief that the figurines were alive. In 1992, Miss Osaka was invited back to Osaka where she received a newly created sister as a present from the Mayor of Osaka. Comparing the three figurines, it is recognizable that they were made at different times.

Color section

No. 11, text, p. 29. *Kyôho-bina*, Emperor (detail); ca. 1750, Kyoto

No. 11, text, p. 29. *Kyôho-bina*, Imperial Couple; ca. 1750, Kyoto

Hina-matsuri/Girls' Festival

No. 13, text, p. 30. *Dairi-bina*, Imperial Couple; ca. 1820-30, Edo (Tokyo); *Kyôho-bina* style, but later

No. 12a, b, text, p. 29/30. *Kyôho-bina*, Emperor; ca. 1800; *Kokin-bina*, Empress; ca. 1830; bought as matching couple

Hina-matsuri/Girls' Festival

No. 14, text, p. 30. *Hina-byôbu* (Two Screens); ca. 1800, Edo (Tokyo)

Hina-matsuri/Girls' Festival

No. 15, text, p. 30. Small Palace with Emperor and Empress, 1880-1900, Kyoto; Peabody Essex Museum

No. 16, text, p. 30. *Kokin-bina*, Imperial Couple, ca. 1890, Kyoto

No. 17, text, p. 30. *Kibori-kimekomi-bina*, Girls' Festival Set; carved wood, *kimekomi* technique, ca. 1910-20, Kyoto

Hina-matsuri/Girls' Festival

No. 18, text, p. 30. Two Guardians; ca. 1850, Edo (Tokyo)

No. 19, text, p. 30. Old Guardian; ca. 1890, Kansai area

No. 20, text, p. 30. Three Court Ladies; ca. 1920, Tokyo

Hina-matsuri/Girls' Festival

No. 21, text, p. 30. Musician; ca. 1830, Edo (Tokyo)

No. 22, text, p. 30. Musician; ca. 1830, Edo (Tokyo)

No. 23, text, p. 30. Three Servants; ca. 1850, Kyoto

Photograph: Roman Szechter

Hina-matsuri/Girls' Festival

No. 24/25, text, p. 30. *Takasago, Ishô-ningyô (Ukiyo-ningyô)*; ca. 1910, Kyoto

Hina-matsuri/Girls' Festival

No. 26, text, p. 30. Procession Carriage of a Court Noble; ca. 1880, Kyoto

No. 27, text, p. 30. Bugaku Dance: *Kochô-no-mai, Ishô-ningyô (Ukiyo-ningyô)*; ca. 1880, Kyoto

Hina-matsuri/Girls' Festival

No. 11, text, p. 29. *Kyôho-bina*, Emperor (detail); ca. 1750, Kyoto

Tango-no-sekku/Boys' Festival

No. 28, text, p. 31. *Musha-ningyô*, Warrior (detail); ca. 1750, Kyoto

Tango-no-sekku/Boys' Festival

No. 30, text, p. 31. *Kazari-uma* (Battle Horse), ca. 1900, Kyoto

No. 29, text, p. 31. *Yoroi-kazari* (Armor and Weapon Display); ca. 1920, Tokyo

Tango-no-sekku/Boys' Festival

No. 28, text, p. 31. *Musha-ningyô* (Warrior and Retainer), ca. 1750, Kyoto

Tango-no-sekku/Boys' Festival

No. 31, text, p. 31. *Musha-ningyô* (Warrior), ca. 1740, Kyoto

Tango-no-sekku/Boys' Festival

No. 33, text, p. 31. *Musha-ningyô* (Young Warrior); ca. 1900, Tokyo

No. 32, text, p. 31: *Musha-ningyô* (Female Warrior); ca. 1800, Kyoto

No. 34, text, p. 31: *Musha-ningyô* (Taikô and Kiyomasa); ca. 1780, Kyoto

Tango-no-sekku/Boys' Festival

No. 35, text, p. 31. Empress Jingû (center), Takenouchi Sukune (right) and Retainer; ca. 1780, Kyoto

Tango-no-sekku/Boys' Festival

No. 36, text, p. 31. Emperor Jimmu in a Fantasy-Style Dress; ca. 1900, Tokyo

Tango-no-sekku/Boys' Festival

No. 37, text, p. 31. *Tengu* King; ca. 1850-80, Tokyo

Tango-no-sekku/Boys' Festival

No. 38, text, p. 31. Emperor Jimmu with Golden Kite Bird; ca. 1890, Tokyo

Tango-no-sekku/Boys' Festival

No. 39, text, p. 31. Kintoki Catching the Carp; ca. 1930-40, Tokyo

No. 40, text, p. 31. Shôki, the Demon Queller; ca. 1900, Tokyo

Ishô-ningyô/Costume Figurines

No. 41, text, p. 32. *Sandai-ningyô*: *Sandai-chigo* (Court-Visiting Figurine); ca. 1800, Kyoto

Ishô-ningyô/Costume Figurines

Photograph: Jeffrey Dykes, courtesy of Peabody Essex Museum, Salem, MA

No. 42, text, p. 32. Small Boy; ca. 1820, Edo; Peabody Essex Museum

No. 43, text, p. 32. Ceremony of Attaining Manhood; ca. 1780, Kyoto

No. 44, text, p. 32. Takeda-style Female Figurine, Parody of a Nô Play (Female Urashima); ca. 1850, Kyoto

Ishô-ningyô/Costume Figurines

No. 45, text, p. 32. Takeda-*ningyô*: Standing Man; ca. 1800, Kyoto

No. 46, text, p. 32. Takeda-*ningyô*: Traveling Priest; ca. 1850, Kyoto

Ishô-ningyô/Costume Figurines

No. 47a, b, text, p. 32. Takeda-*ningyô*: Two Fighting Heroes, ca. 1830, Kyoto

Ishô-ningyô/Costume Figurines

No. 48, text, p. 32. Sumô Wrestler; ca. 1860-80, Kyoto

No. 49, text, p. 32. Tea Master; ca. 1900, Kyoto

Ishô-ningyô/Costume Figurines

No. 50, text, p. 32. Child Dancer of the Nô Play, *Sambasô*; ca. 1850, Edo (Tokyo)

Ishô-ningyô/Costume Figurines

No. 51, text, p. 32. Fashion Figurine: Young lady of the Mid-Edo Period; ca. 1780, Kyoto

Ishô-ningyô/Costume Figurines

No. 53, text, p. 32. Three Female Musicians; ca. 1800, Edo (Tokyo)

No. 52, text, p. 32. Three-fold Fashion Figurine With Change of Kimono; ca. 1790, Kyoto

Ishô-ningyô/Costume Figurines

No. 54, text, p. 33. Lantern Shop; ca. 1900, Tokyo; Peabody Essex Museum

Ishô-ningyô/Costume Figurines

No. 55a, b, text, p. 33. Three-fold Fashion Figurine with Changeable Wigs; ca. 1900, Kyoto

Ishô-ningyô/Costume Figurines

No. 56, text, p. 33. Imperial Wedding; 1924, Kyoto

Ishô-ningyô/Costume Figurines

No. 57, text, p. 33. Costume Figurine; after 1945

No. 59, text, p. 33. *Hagoromo*, Nô Play; ca. 1960

No. 58, text, p. 33. Courtesan; 1955, Osaka; Museum of the City of New York

Photograph: courtesy of Museum of the City of New York

73

Ishô-ningyô/Costume Figurines

No. 60, text, p. 33. "*Mizura-gami*" (Boy in Heian-Period Dress); ca. 1880, Kyoto

Gosho-ningyô/Imperial Palace Figurines

No. 61, text, p. 33. *Gosho-ningyô* with Kimono (detail); ca. 1780, Kyoto

No. 61, text, p. 33. *Gosho-ningyô* with Kimono; ca. 1780, Kyoto

Gosho-ningyô/Imperial Palace Figurines

No. 62, text, p. 33. *Gosho-ningyô* Holding a Rope; ca. 1830, Kyoto

No. 61, see left page. *Gosho-ningyô* (undressed)

No. 63, text, p. 33. Holding the Spring Horse; ca. 1830, Kyoto

Gosho-ningyô/Imperial Palace Figurines

No. 64, text, p. 33. Parody of Daikoku, the God of Wealth; ca. 1880-90, Kyoto

No. 65, text, p. 33. Mechanical Figurine: Holding the Spring Horse; ca. 1830, Kyoto

No. 66, text, p. 33. Mechanical Figurine: Parody of a Lion Dance; 19th c., Kyoto

Gosho-ningyô/Imperial Palace Figurines

No. 67, text, p. 33. Mechanical Figurine: Boy with *Eboshi* Cap and *Denden* Drum; 19th c., Kyoto

Gosho-ningyô/Imperial Palace Figurines

No. 68, text, p. 33. Figurine as a Child of the Warrior Class on Horseback; ca. 1840, Kyoto

Gosho-ningyô/Imperial Palace Figurines

No. 73, text, p. 34. Crawling Baby; ca. 1900, Kyoto

No. 72, text, p. 33. "Commoner's Topknot"; ca. 1830, Kyoto

Nos. 69, 70, 71, text, p. 33. *Denden* Drum Holder, Crawling Baby, Drummer; ca. 1850, Kansai area

Gosho-ningyô/Imperial Palace Figurines

No. 74, text, p. 34. Parody of a Nô Play; ca. 1830, Kyoto

No. 75, text, p. 34. Parody of the Kabuki Play, *Yanone*; ca. 1800-50, Kyoto

Gosho-ningyô/Imperial Palace Figurines

No. 76, text, p. 34. Two Children from the Warrior Class; ca. 1820, Kyoto

Gosho-ningyô/Imperial Palace Figurines

No. 77a, b, text, p. 34. Two Children of the Warrior Class; ca. 1850, Kyoto

Gosho-ningyô/Imperial Palace Figurines

No. 78, text, p. 34. Play Doll for Children of the Nobility; ca. 1800, Kyoto

No. 79, text, p. 34. Two Children of the Court Aristocracy; ca. 1900-20, Kyoto

Gosho-ningyô/Imperial Palace Figurines

No. 80, text, p. 34. Standing Boy with Commoner's Hairstyle; ca. 1840-50, Kyoto

No. 81, text, p. 34. Standing Dressed Boy; ca. 1850, Kyoto

Ichimatsu-*ningyô*/Iki-*ningyô*

No. 82, text, p. 34. Ichimatsu-*ningyô*: Urban Commoner's Child; ca. 1840, Kyoto

No. 83, text, p. 34. Ichimatsu-*ningyô*: Little Boy; ca. 1900-20, Tokyo

Ichimatsu-*ningyô*/Iki-*ningyô*

No. 84, text, p. 34. Ichimatsu-*ningyô*: Little Boy with Dragonfly Hairstyle; ca. 1900, Tokyo

Ichimatsu-*ningyô*/Iki-*ningyô*

No. 85, text, p. 34. Life-size Figures: Peasant Mother and Child; ca. 1880, Tokyo; Peabody Essex Museum

Ichimatsu-*ningyô*/*Iki-ningyô*

No. 86, text, p. 34. Friendship Dolls; 1928, 1989; The Newark Museum

FRIENDS OF JAPAN SOCIETY GALLERY

Ingrid Arneberg
Mr. and Mrs. Peter A. Aron
Mr. and Mrs. Armand P. Bartos
Phillip C. Broughton
Mary Griggs Burke
Mr. and Mrs. Willard G. Clark
Mr. and Mrs. Theodore R. Conant
Mr. and Mrs. C. Douglas Dillon
Mrs. Frederick L. Ehrman
Mrs. Myron S. Falk, Jr.
Mr. and Mrs. Hart Fessenden
Dr. and Mrs. Roger Gerry
Mr. and Mrs. Charles A. Greenfield
Louis W. Hill, Jr.
Liza Hyde
Noriko Ishikawa
Dr. and Mrs. Sebastian Izzard
Maurice M. Kawashima
Mr. and Mrs. James J. Lally
Lucia Woods Lindley
Mrs. Jean Chisholm Lindsey
Mr. and Mrs. Henry A. Loeb
Mr. and Mrs. Leighton R. Longhi
Mr. and Mrs. Morton H. Meyerson
Suzanne R. Mitchell
Klaus F. Naumann
Houn Ohara
Mr. and Mrs. Alex Pagel
Etsuya Sasazu
Mr. and Mrs. Soshitsu Sen
Mr. and Mrs. Stephen A. Simon
Mr. and Mrs. Alan J. Strassman
Mr. and Mrs. Donald B. Straus
Roger and Kathleen Weston

ART ADVISORY COMMITTEE

Richard S. Lanier
Chairman

Barbara Ford
Roger Goepper
Oliver Impey
Sherman E. Lee
Julia Meech
Samuel C. Morse
Miyeko Murase
Robert M. Murdock
Hiroko Nishida
Valrae Reynolds
John M. Rosenfield
Emily J. Sano
Yoshiaki Shimizu
Henry Trubner

ADVISORY COMMITTEE ON CARE
AND HANDLING

Sondra Castile
Conservatorial Consultant

Mitsuhiro Abe
Takemitsu Oba

BOARD OF DIRECTORS OF THE JAPAN SOCIETY

Hodding Carter, II
E. Gerald Corrigan
Yoshitaka Fujitani
Louis V. Gerstner, Jr.
William H. Gleysteen, Jr.
Carol Gluck
William H. Gray
Maurice R. Greenberg
Koji Hirao
Tsuneo Iwasaki
Richard S. Lanier
Deryck C. Maughan
Ira M. Millstein
Jiro Murase
Takeshi Nagaya
Shin Nakahara
Yoshinobu Nishikawa
Hugh Patrick
Peter G. Peterson
John M. Rosenfield
Mikio Sasaki
Michael P. Schulhof
Masataka Shimasaki
Michael I. Sovern
Mineo Sugiyama
Richard A Voell
Paul A Volcker
Goro Watanabe
Daniel Yankelovich

OFFICERS OF THE JAPAN SOCIETY

Michael I. Sovern
Chairman

Goro Watanabe
Vice Chairman

William H. Gleysteen, Jr.
President

John K. Wheeler
Vice President

Carl E. Schellhorn
Vice President, Finance & Administration

Richard L. Huber
Treasurer

Alice Young
Secretary

Iris Harris
Assistant Secretary